JOURNOLISTS

JOHN KOSKI is Associate Editor of *YOU* Magazine. His life is a constant struggle against listlessness.

MITCHELL SYMONS is a former BBC TV director who writes for a variety of publications, including a regular column in *Punch*. As well as writing lists, he devises television game shows and compiles fiendishly difficult crosswords.

1991

John Koski and Mitchell Symons

Cartoons by Ian Dicks

CHAPMANS

Chapmans Publishers Ltd
141–143 Drury Lane
London WC2B 5TB

First published by Chapmans 1991

ISBN 1–85592–713–6

A CIP catalogue record for this book
is available from the British Library

Photoset in Linotron Times by
MC Typeset Ltd, Wouldham, Rochester, Kent
Printed and bound in Great Britain by
Clays Ltd, St Ives plc

ACKNOWLEDGEMENTS

Welcome to the third *YOU* Magazine book of *Journolists*. Special thanks are due to Sara Driver and Patricia Martin for their tireless research and to our four most invaluable contributors: Malcolm Burgess, Donnie Kerr, Steve Clothier and John Machin.

PICTURE CREDITS

All the photographs are reproduced by courtesy of Associated Newspapers plc, except for: BBC TV News, p. 20; Thames Television, p. 31; BBC Television, p. 59.

The publishers acknowledge the rights of the copyright holders in the illustrations throughout this work.

CONTENTS

The ten ages of disillusionment

Babyhood: *Discovering that you have to be trained to do what you happily did naturally*

Childhood: *Finding out that your best friend likes Teenage Mutant Ninja Turtles*

Teenagehood: *Realising that Adrian Mole has said it all*

Twentysomething: *Facing the fact that you've got to go to work for the rest of your life*

Thirtysomething: *Discovering that the records you want are always in the cut-price section*

Fortysomething: *Learning that people couldn't care less about the Sixties*

Fiftysomething: *Desperately telling yourself that you are still younger than Joan Collins*

Sixtysomething: *Realising that you are as old as Dot in* EastEnders

Seventysomething: *Discovering that your youth is the subject of a historic theme park*

Eightysomething: *Giving up on television, because you can't hear the sound and can't see the teletext subtitles*

The drinks vending machine dispenses only hot water (no change there)

Company cars are replaced by Red Rover bus passes

Is your company in trouble? Ten tell-tale signs

The sales director starts entertaining clients at Spud-U-Like

This year's advertising campaign is on the back of bus tickets

The water cooler has algae in it

The Red Cross takes over the running of the staff canteen

The photocopier works

The finance director spends all day under the desk sucking his thumb

You discover the managing director steaming stamps off envelopes

There's a whip-round whenever the paperclips run out

You can't fight the system – ten examples of its spreading influence

'Shaving system': *Twin-bladed razor*

'In-car entertainment system': *Radio cassette player*

'Dental protection system': *Fluoride toothpaste in a pump pack*

'Personal organisation system': *Diary*

'Shelving system': *Shelves*

'Office system': *Colour co-ordinated desk, chair and filing cabinet*

'Climate control system': *Air conditioning*

'Home protection system': *Leave a light on when you go out*

'Lawn care system': *Sprinkler*

'Storage system': *Cupboard*

Hope against expectation – ten examples

Returning an entry for a *Reader's Digest* prize draw

Staying for the second half of a Tanita Tikaram concert

Joining a health club

Getting married for a second time

Checking the Saturday night TV schedules

Asking if service is included

Going on a camping holiday in Scotland

Taking something you bought for £1 to *The Antiques Roadshow*

Buying a ticket for the fifth day of an England v West Indies Test Match

Planting shrubs from a garden centre

Personal interests – a guide to that bit at the bottom of job application forms

'Reading, especially modern novels': *Took* First Among Equals *on holiday*

'Current affairs': *Reads the newspapers*

'Photography': *Takes pictures with no people in them*

LANDSCAPE SEASCAPE

SNOWSCAPE MOUNTAINSCAPE

'Sport': *Stays awake for the final of the World Snooker Championships*

'Modern cinema': *Member of a video club*

'Decorative arts': *Does own wallpapering*

'Debating': *Enjoys an argument in the pub*

'Politics': *Votes in local elections*

'Nature conservation': *Gardening*

'Travel': *Takes holidays abroad*

Beyond arachnophobia! Ten new fears

Kenlophobia: *Fear of being hungry two hours after eating in a Chinese restaurant*

Yugophobia: *Fear of being last in line for a company car*

Phonophobia: *Fear of being caught singing along to 'hold the line' music*

Anoraknaphobia: *Fear of train spotters*

Robophobia: *Fear of being taken to see an Arnold Schwarzenegger film*

Digestophobia: *Fear of having your name chosen by a computer*

Plugophobia: *Fear of being invited on* Aspel

Jackophobia: *Fear of plastic surgery*

Yoyophobia: *Fear that everything eventually makes a comeback*

Omophobia: *Fear of post-ironing smells*

Ten nightmares for the 1990s

Breaching the 21-unit barrier by Tuesday lunchtime

Oliver Reed and George Best on the same *Wogan* show

French & Saunders workout videos

BHS introduces a Duchess of York fashion range

Tripe is proved to be the only safe food to eat

An ozone layer memorial service

Joan Collins in *The Stud II*

The wrong kind of snow blows into the Channel Tunnel

Norman Schwarzkopf in The Gulf War II

Eric Clapton does 365 nights at the Albert Hall

Community service – ten useful alternatives to prison

Standing between Muriel Gray and the camera

Acting as a decoy for opinion pollsters

Caddying for paperboys on Sunday mornings

Running a street theatre vigilante group

Acting as an interpreter for British Rail announcers

Standing in for Terry Wogan

Invigilating garage mechanics

Prodding junior hospital doctors whenever they doze off

Re-setting digital watches when the clocks go back

Checking there's always paper in pub toilets

A quick guide to evening classes

'Aerobics': *Dancing to old Lulu records*
'Hostess cookery': *Discovering vol-au-vents*
'Car maintenance': *The big end explained*
'Car maintenance for women': *The big end on a Mini explained*
'Holiday French': *Learning to say* 'Parlez-vous Anglais?'
'Commerce': *Typing*
'Pottery': *Endlessly producing ashtrays for friends*
'Writing workshop': *People reading out their embarrassing poems*
'Small business skills': *How to fill in a VAT return*
'Self-defence': *Learning to turn a rolled-up newspaper into a lethal weapon*

'Let's run it up the flagpole' – a guide to business-speak

'We're on a learning curve': *We don't know what we're doing*
'Let's put it on the back burner': *I can't be bothered to talk about it now*
'Let's do lunch': *Let's waste each other's time at someone else's expense*
'Let's push the concept to the limits': *Let's go on talking about nothing until it's time for lunch*
'Do you have a window in your diary?': *Can I see you?*
'I'll get back to you': *No, I won't*
'Let me run this one by you one more time': *It's still too early for lunch*
'Let's put that one on ice': *Forget it*
'It's a toe-dipping exercise': *I won't get fired if it goes wrong*
'Shall we touch base next week?': *Dinner?*

Ten modern labours of Hercules

Make Kenny Dalglish laugh uncontrollably
Get a builder to accept payment by cheque
Devise a new way to package Morecambe and Wise repeats
Sell a flat in London's Docklands
Find a decent Scottish goalkeeper
Mount a successful 'Nicholas Ridley for Foreign Secretary' campaign
Come up with a new excuse for speeding
Find Prince Edward a proper job
Write a witty British sitcom
Sell a story on the exchange rate mechanism of the European Monetary System to *Sunday Sport*

Beyond the everlasting lightbulb – ten products the world is waiting for

A microwave fridge for quick-chilling beer

A £3.99 aerial which picks up programmes from next door's satellite dish

A cream cracker that doesn't break when you butter it

A remote control which turns down the volume of the kids

A personal stereo jamming device

A boil-in-the-bag candlelit dinner for two

Self-cleaning oven gloves

Rap records which are audible only to people under the age of fourteen

A magnet for picking up cat hairs

Charity collector repellent

The ten laws of bus travel

At least five buses go by in the opposite direction before yours arrives

The one day you have the exact fare is the day it goes up

If you hail a taxi, your bus trundles into view as you get in

If you're at the front of the queue, the driver comes to a halt at the back

The more crowded the bus, the more likely you'll be carrying a newly bought duvet

The stationary bus you've run for won't move for another fifteen minutes

Buses turn up within seconds of your lighting a cigarette

It's still a mystery why three turn up at once

Nobody ever gives up their seat for you

If you start to walk, a bus appears when you are exactly half-way between stops

Weekender-speak – a guide to interpretation

'We like to think of this as our real home': *We feel guilty about having two houses*

'Of course we contribute to village life': *We paid the poll tax, didn't we?*

'We buy as much as we can locally': *Milk and bread*

'You must come out and visit us': *Nobody here will talk to us*

'It can be difficult to get the basics': *No monkfish*

'We try to fit in with the local community': *We don't carry around Sainsbury's shopping bags*

'It's great for re-charging the batteries': *And after driving for five hours on a Friday night, you need to re-charge your batteries*

'The local pub is full of characters': *Weekenders with different jobs from ours*

'It's a much healthier way of living': *We occasionally go for walks*

'We're not against rural development': *We just don't want them building a council estate in our village*

Ten places where we have yet to see advertisements

Policemen's helmets

Princess Eugenie's pram

Paul Gascoigne's thighs

Hearses

The Queen Mother's hat

Fire engines

Streakers' chests

Postage stamps

The Archbishop of Canterbury's mitre

Envelopes from the Inland Revenue

Making sense of school prospectuses

'Extensive playing fields': *Property developers, please note*

'Parental involvement encouraged': *Roped in for fund-raising activities*

'Reputation for drama': *Usually in the staff room*

'Aim to develop fully rounded students': *Poor exam results*

'Wide range of extra-curricular activities': *Sponsored walks to buy books*

'Relaxed atmosphere': *Skateboarding in the corridors*

'Traditional teaching methods': *History master works from notes he made thirty years ago*

'Staff work as a team': *Headmaster usually having a nervous breakdown*

'Strong on sports': *Ray of hope for dim pupils*

'Modern teaching methods': *Classroom riots*

Ten ways to get rich quick

Record a pop song which is banned by the BBC

Follow John McEnroe around with a swear box

Have an industrial accident in America

Discover a cure for *That's Life*

Take five pairs of Levi's to Moscow

Write a book about your experiences in British Intelligence

Charge the runners in the London Marathon a toll to cross Westminster Bridge

Be the official supplier of sliced limes to bars selling Mexican beer

Divorce Steven Spielberg (Warning: you have to marry him first)

Be awarded the Department of Transport traffic cone concession

Things ain't what they used to be – ten examples

'Business park': *Industrial estate*

'Quality time': *Playing with the kids*

'Leisure centre': *Swimming pool with two Space Invader machines*

'Work station': *Desk*

'Remuneration package': *Salary plus company car*

'Rationalisation': *Job cuts*

'Holiday centre': *Caravan site with shop*

'Theme park': *Pleasure beach which isn't on the coast*

'Contract doorman': *Bouncer*

'Financial consultant': *Insurance salesman*

Ten new gadgets for that dream kitchen

A muesli disposal unit

A musical chip pan fire alarm

Built-in biscuit tins

A baked bean storage tank

An automatic money-off coupon filing and retrieval system

A boiled cabbage extractor fan

A non-stick floor

A black hole which swallows up those ancient tins of peaches in heavy syrup

A solar-powered tin opener

A hand-held vacuum cleaner for toast crumbs

Bones of contention – ten things couples can never work out

Who gets stuck holding the programme at the theatre

Who sits by the window on a plane

Whose turn it is to drive home from a party

Who gets the aisle seat at the cinema

Who should record the answering machine message

Who holds whom round the waist while dancing

Who gets to read the newspaper first in the morning

Whose parents should be visited on Christmas Day and whose on Boxing Day

Who should take the rubbish out

Who checked that the front door is locked

Ten products to complete that dream bathroom

A 'Snigger-Your-Weight' bath mat

A chime toilet

A heated toothbrush rack

A knee-high newspaper reading stand

A mirror which doesn't reflect morning-after-the-night-before eyes

A jacuzzi with Force 9 gale tidal wave facility

A combined personal stereo and shower cap

A voice-activated answering machine with a variety of replies to the question: 'Are you going to be in there all day?'

A fully retractable loo seat

A three-tap sink – hot, cold and liver salts

Ten health scares for the 1990s

Citycosis: *Sick-as-a-parrot syndrome suffered by redundant stockbrokers*

American Measles: *Delusion that you can knock spots off everyone else*

Delirium Hemens: *Madness affecting bodybuilders*

Scarlet Fever: *Aversion to deejays who play* Lady in Red *at the end of the night*

White Cholera: *Anxiety induced by dealing with bureaucracy*

Hay Fever: *Irritation caused by the dust in second-hand bookshops*

Annaemia: *Loss of interest in Anne Diamond's career*

Arthuritis: *Irrational desire to appear in a Tesco commercial*

Green Jaundice: *Condition caused by over-exposure to ecological issues*

Ninjavitis: *Trembling at how much you have to spend on the kids' birthday presents*

Heritage centres – a guide for visitors

'See how your ancestors lived': *In a fibreglass cave with Jean-Michel Jarre music piped in*

'Authentic atmosphere': *Smells like the drains are blocked*

'Our rich island story': *Twenty wax dummies in different period costumes*

'History comes alive': *Oliver Cromwell's head moves*

'Eavesdrop on typical conversations': *Tape of lots of people who sound like Eddie Grundy*

'Perfect for children': *Large array of torture devices*

'Exciting audio-visual experience': *Slide show with commentary every fifteen minutes*

'Historically accurate': *No Ninja Turtles in Elizabeth I's court*

'Centrepiece': *Ye olde souvenir shoppe*

'Be transported into the past': *Apart from the prices*

Ten great trials of life
David Attenborough missed

Getting the last drop of ketchup out of a bottle

Using a cash dispenser while surrounded by skinheads

Grating the last bit of cheese without skinning your finger

Trying to talk coherently to a telephone answering machine

Tearing clingfilm

Putting toner into a photocopying machine

Disposing of Christmas trees

Recovering from the full English breakfast in hotels

Getting a refund from British Rail for an unused ticket

Trying to find a pen in a bank

We do like to be beside the seaside: a guide to British resorts

'Miles of deserted beaches': *Nuclear power station nearby*

'Heritage coastline': *Footpath on top of the cliffs*

'Plenty to do in all weathers': *Pubs open all day*

'Traditional': *Plastic lemonade bottles stuck in the sand*

'Noted for seafood': *Fish and chips in a polystyrene tray*

'Noted for traditional seafood': *Fish and chips in newspaper*

'English Riviera': *English weather, Riviera prices*

'Unspoilt': *Where's the amusement arcade?*

'Seaside entertainment': *Bingo*

'Safe': *Nobody dares to go in the sea because of pollution*

Ten ways to spot a bachelor

Fridge empty except for two bottles of Grolsch and half a tub of taramasalata

Doesn't need to buy a dog to go to the pub

Owns two-and-a-half place settings (unmatched)

Bank balance in the black

Has never heard the phrase 'I've got a headache'

Arrives at work each day from a different direction

Buys totally useless gadgets

Rubbish bin overflowing with takeaway curry containers

Two dirty glasses and a promotional coffee mug permanently in the sink

Grey bed sheets

Well, if you want to know what *I* think . . .

Taxi driver-speak — a guide to interpretation

'In some ways you've got to admire the bloke': *Saddam Hussein*

'I'll cut round the back to avoid the traffic': *I'll double the length of your journey*

'Sorry, mate, it's out of my way': *I'm not here for your convenience, y'know*

'Haven't you got anything smaller?': *Why don't I just keep the change?*

'Is there a route you'd prefer me to take?': *Or can I take you for a ride?*

'If you want my opinion . . .': *Too bad, you're going to get it anyway*

'They should string 'em all up': *This is the only part of 'The Knowledge' I can remember*

'Ten miles the other side of town? Certainly': *I wish the American tourists would come back*

'I don't know what the world's coming to': *Why doesn't the government ban minicabs?*

'Where do you want to go?': *This is just the opening gambit in our negotiations*

Police-speak – a guide to interpretation

'Do you realise what speed you were doing, sir?': *I always love this bit*

'I'm all in favour of putting the bobby back on the beat': *As long as I can keep my desk job*

'Come off it, sarge': *I should be in* The Bill

'Right, you're nicked!': *I wish they'd bring back* The Sweeney

'There was an incident involving firearms outside a bank, as a result of which two men were fatally wounded': *We shot two bank robbers*

'A man is currently helping us with our inquiries': *Gotcha!*

'We can only do our job with the consent of the community': *The record crime figures are your fault*

'Community policing': *Dancing with a big black lady at the Notting Hill Carnival*

''Ello, 'ello, 'ello, what's the meaning of this then?: *Why shouldn't I have a catchphrase?*

'Can I refer to my notes, m'lud?': *The ones I made five minutes ago*

Are you in line for redundancy? Ten tell-tale signs

You're the only one who didn't get a desk diary

The managing director's secretary bursts into tears whenever she sees you

Your desk is moved into the toilet

You are invited to a surprise farewell party (yours)

The tea lady stops giving you sugar

They stop paying you

Your boss turns down your offer to buy him lunch next week

The company moves to Peterborough without telling you

You find government retraining brochures stuffed into your coat pockets

You are asked for a full breakdown of your paperclip usage over the past year

The ten laws of shop changing-rooms

You bounce off the walls like a pinball when trying on trousers

You always wonder if you can manage without taking off your shoes

There is only ever one hook

There are no hangers

However carefully you draw the curtain, there is a gap at one side or the other

There is always a gap at the bottom of the curtain

A shop assistant always says 'How are you doing in there?' when you're half-dressed

You have to back out of the cubicle to see yourself properly in the mirror

The hessian-style wall-covering always has a triangular rip in it

Even the smallest cubicle is better than a communal changing-room

Ten things which lurk in everyone's kitchen cupboards

A jar containing one slice of pickled beetroot

Two sachets of British Airways sugar

A gnarled tube of tomato puree

A jar of Rose's Lime Marmalade with penicillin topping

A sachet of Little Chef brown sauce

A jar of an aged relative's homemade chutney (unopened)

An almost complete jar of cheddar cheese spread with a free tea-towel offer which expired three years ago

A tin of octopus brought back as a joke from a 1982 holiday

A dog-eared packet of cornflour (half-used)

A tin of sardines with the key missing

Ten updated quotes for St Valentine's Day

It is better to have loved and lost than never to have been on *Blind Date*

Greater love hath no man than this, that he lay down a patio for his neighbour

How do I love thee? Let me count the bills

All is fair in love and the January sales

If music be the food of love, why can't I manage more than a three-minute pop song?

Je t'aime . . . Moi nonplussed

Love will find a way – but so will letters from the tax man

All you need is love – and a generous expense account

Money can't buy me love . . . does you does or does you don't take Access?

Roses are red, violets are blue. Is that all I'm worth – flowers?

Lor, worra billy doo!

That exam for seven-year-olds: ten sample questions

Contextualise Noddy's relationship with Big Ears in the light of non-heterosexist values

'If the Royal Mail were privatised, there would be no role for Postman Pat's black-and-white cat.' Discuss

Design an alternative to the Channel Tunnel using only a Fairy Liquid bottle, a pipe cleaner and some sticky-backed plastic

What is the chemical formula for a stink bomb?

Outline the arguments for and against giving Thomas the Tank Engine a government subsidy

If Desperate Dan eats five cow pies a day for ten years, what are his chances of contracting BSE?

Explain Phillip Schofield (extra marks will be given for diagrams)

Describe the physiological processes which are likely to occur if you eat a dozen Cadbury's Creme Eggs, three Mars choc ices and a packet of wine gums

What effect has the feminist movement had on Barbie and Sindy?

Is there still a place for conkers in the video game age?

Diet-speak – a guide to interpretation

'Super dietary supplement': *Resembles toxic waste*

'Discovered by the Aztecs': *You don't see many fat Aztecs around, do you?*

'Totally natural': *Water*

'Slimming secrets': *Eat less*

'First time in Britain': *Previously banned*

'Developed by top scientists': *Expensive*

'Vitality diet': *Green salads*

'Wonder diet': *Being investigated by the Department of Health*

'Eat-what-you-like diet': *In dolls' tea party proportions*

'Total dieting system': *Includes piece of paper to keep a note of your weight*

Ten signs of a middle-class recession

Hampstead to St John's Wood hunger marches by unemployed nannies

The price of free-range eggs tumbles

No queues for the ski lifts

Drinking tap water becomes fashionable

Volvo sales plummet

Libraries have to take on extra staff

Fast food chains accept American Express

Country house hotels are converted into old people's homes

Phone calls are answered eagerly by West End theatre box offices

Either the ballet lessons or the pony have to go

Ten things you only do in an hotel

Happily pay £1.50 for the tiny bag of pistachio nuts in the mini-bar
Eat breakfast, lunch, afternoon tea and dinner in the same day
Watch *Kilroy*
Smile at people you don't know
Agonise about not being able to clean the bath
Press your trousers
Carefully hang up all your clothes
Leave the TV set on standby all night
Use a shower cap
Use the hand towels as facecloths

The new country code

All roads lead to the folk museum
Range Rovers have the right to force you off the road
Devon cream teas are available everywhere
The biggest mansions are owned by religious cults
All footpaths end with a barbed wire fence
Behind every conservationist is a worried homeowner
Behind every neighbourhood watch is a worried weekender
Archaeological digs signal the imminent construction of a superstore
Traditional country fayres must feature an inflatable castle
Labi Siffre headlines at the local arts festival

Are you a man or a mouse? Ten tell-tale signs

You never get to use the arm rest on cinema seats
You are intimidated by flag-day sellers
Old ladies push in front of you in queues
The kids tell you when to go to bed
You find Rice Krispies a little too loud
There is only one woman in your life – your mother
You get seasick on boating lakes
You've never bought a car for less than the asking price
You still have a name tag sewn into your anorak
You never go out in winter without cotton wool in your ears

Esther: Final Court of Appeal

Consumerist-speak – a guide to interpretation

'Consumer': *One born every minute*
'Hidden dangers': *Car manufacturers fail to warn you against driving off a cliff*
'Be assertive': *Ask if there's a guarantee*
'Job for an expert': *Changing a plug*
'Final right of redress': *Threaten to call Esther Rantzen*
'The law is on your side': *Not that it will do you much good*
'Read the small print': *Then get someone to explain it to you*
'Use common sense': *Don't fall for self-squeezing sponges*
'Be questioning': *Ask yourself if Taiwan is renowned for antique Staffordshire figures*
'Know your rights': *Learn to read*

'Could I have five minutes of your time?' Ten replies to get rid of market researchers

'Only if I can have £5 of your money?'

'Qué?'

'Certainly, would 8.30–8.35 am on 28 November be convenient?'

'I'm afraid I've signed the Official Secrets Act'

'Okay, but no funny business – I've got a gun'

'Woof-woof woof-woof woof-woof'

'You'll have to speak to my agent'

'Have you got a licence for that clipboard?'

'I was just going to ask you the same thing'

'I only consider requests like that in writing'

Is the world really getting warmer? Ten portents to look out for

Swarms of hand-held fans over Britain

An EC double-glazing mountain (Everest)

An EC anti-freeze lake

The introduction of fridge-freezers with sleeping compartments

Watford-on-Sea

A boom in package holidays to the Yukon

Baked Alaska

Michael Fish tells us not to worry, global warming isn't on the way

Barbecueing the turkey at Christmas

Solar-powered toothbrushes

Beyond the strippergram – ten ideas they're working on

The Diagram (bashful beauty in low-heeled shoes turns up to shake your hand)

The Cardiogram (avuncular breakfast TV presenter arrives and takes his cardie off)

The Milligram (pop star sings *My Boy Lollipop*)

The Cablegram (media tycoon forces you to watch movies you've never heard of)

The Kilogram (Middle East dictator invades your home uninvited)

The Phonogram (pushy person rings up and asks if you've ever thought what would happen to your family if you died)

The Anagram (regal lady in headscarf tells you to 'naff off')

The Oscillogram (shrill-voiced TV star shouts 'Surprise, surprise' through the letter-box)

The Cryptogram (tweedy type arrives and finishes off your newspaper crossword)

The Epigram (cast of thousands whisks you away on a sponsored walk to the Promised Land)

Ten reasons not to work out

Picture yourself in a leotard

Didn't the bloke who invented jogging die of a heart attack?

It's much more satisfying to develop the mind

All those Huey Lewis records they play in gyms

Somebody's bound to discover it's bad for you

What's so great about being able to run up stairs?

It's so narcissistic

You'll make all your friends feel inadequate

Arnold Schwarzenegger has said it all, really

Carrying a sports bag around is so inconvenient

And mine's a spaghetti à la Kalashnikov

Ten ways to live dangerously

Have a working lunch with Kate Adie
Arrest Zsa Zsa Gabor
Smile at people on the Underground
Wear a Union Jack T-shirt in Glasgow
Ask the cab driver if he'll take a cheque
Dress up as a hedgehog and hitch-hike on the A1
Beat your boss in the company golf tournament
Go swimming off a British beach
Take a driving lesson in central Birmingham
Eat garlic bread before a job interview

Ten green products we're waiting for

Low-fat Northern comedians
Sugar-free episodes of *The Waltons*
High moral fibre politicians
Additive-free Olympic athletes
Biodegradable soap operas
Telephone directories without E numbers
Free-range egg cups
Fully returnable chat show guests
Preservative-free Hollywood stars
Non-recycled TV schedules

Ten proverbs for a cynical age

Cleanliness is next to impossible
Never put off till tomorrow what you can do the
  day after
It's better to travel hopefully than to stay put
All roads lead to an impenetrable one-way system
You can't have your cake and keep your figure
People shouldn't live in glass houses
If the mountain won't come to Mohammed, sod it
An unwatched pot boils over
Don't worry, it's already happened
An apple a day keeps the greengrocer happy

Marketing-speak – a guide to interpretation

'Retail outlet': *Shop*
'Point of sale': *Inside shop*
'Corporate image': *Key rings bearing the company logo*
'Human resources': *Staff*
'Product development': *Legless turkeys*
'Purchasing power': *Money*
'Added value': *Free recipe book*
'Premium-priced': *Overpriced*
'Lifestyle': *Hobbies*
'Consumer': *Housewife*

Ten things always found in car glove compartments

An empty tin of travel sweets
A ten-year-old AA Handbook
A broken tape
A dozen petrol coupons which are now invalid
A pair of cheap sunglasses
A Little Chef map of Britain
An A–Z Guide with at least twenty pages missing
A torch with corroded batteries
A bit of plastic which has fallen off the car interior
No gloves

Ten people who make us suspicious

Celebrities who go on *Wogan* without anything to promote

Men who carry portable phones at weekends

Children who don't read comics

Holidaymakers who don't take up their full allocation of duty-frees

Rock groups who refuse to play live

Parents who never let their children eat sweets

Women who wear make-up on the beach

People who read Proust on the Tube

Salesmen who wear polyester flares

Politicians who call interviewers by their first names

Is age creeping up on you? Ten danger signs

Chief Constables start to look younger

You go to bed earlier than your children

You find yourself looking forward to *That's Life*

You tell your son to do something about his hair

You can't remember why you found *Monty Python* funny

You realise you've spent more years working than you did at school

You think life insurance salesmen are worth listening to

You avoid subtracting your age from 70

You actually do 'check with your doctor' before doing exercise

You skip the office party

Don't worry about those flight cancellations – ten reasons to spend your holiday at Gatwick Airport

The newspapers don't cost £2 a copy

The restaurants are better than those in Greece

Airports don't crash

The kids like sleeping on plastic seats

Think of the money you'll save on suntan lotion

You won't have to send postcards

You might be interviewed by a TV news crew

Mosquitoes are not a problem

It doesn't matter if you lose your passport

You can manage without a phrase book

Ten recipes from the Mad Cow Cookbook

Silly Con Carne
T-Brained Steak
Potty Roast
Cannelooni
Meathead Loaf
Lasagneurotic
Steak Ta Ta
Going Spare Rib
Cottage Hospital Pie
Beef Napoleon

On the twelfth day of Christmas, my true love gave to me . . .

Twelve lords a-sleeping
Eleven ladies lunching
Ten portable phones piping
Nine drum machines drumming
Eight maids a-metering
Seven Swan drinkers a-swigging
Six Gazzas playing
Five Amex gold cards
Four cold-calling nerds
Three battery hens
Two Ninja Turtles
And a partridge in a reduced pear sauce

The big Christmas build-up — ten warning signs

Radio stations start playing Slade
You can't move for Old Spice ads on TV
The dustmen cheerfully take away all your rubbish
Everybody says 'It doesn't feel like Christmas'
Vacuum cleaners are draped in tinsel in electricity showrooms
Queen release a Greatest Hits album
Cookery pages have 'Why Not Try Duck This Year?' features
'We must get together in the New Year' becomes a catchphrase
The BBC unearths a 'lost' Goon Show episode which is to be the highlight of its Boxing Day programming
People start to remind you of your behaviour at last year's office party

Ten naff Christmas presents for women

Ginger tights
Supermarket own-label talcum powder
Padded coat hangers
Miniature thermometers
Knitted dolls to cover toilet rolls
Bowls of assorted bulbs
A set of non-stick pans
A book of *Monty Python* scripts
A box of Matchmakers
A foot spa

The true meaning of Christmas

Christmas tradition: *Queueing up at M&S to exchange unwanted presents*

Christmas spirit: *Secretaries being sick on the way home from office parties*

Christmas pudding: *Russell Grant in a duvet-sized sweater*

Christmas box: *Television*

Christmas bonus: *Politicians are off the TV screens*

Christmas message: *'Minimum payment should reach us by 08/01/92'*

Christmas service: *Impossible to catch the barman's eye*

Christmas carol: *'I Believe in Father Christmas' by Greg Lake*

Christmas decoration: *Awarded for gluttony above and beyond the call of duty*

Christmas card: *'You were out when we tried to deliver a parcel'*

Tough at the top

Boxing Day party-speak – a guide to interpretation

'Have you come far?': *Let's get the M25 over with*

'There's some food coming round in a minute': *Ingenious ways with turkey leftovers*

'We had a fairly quiet Christmas Day': *Twelve hours slumped in front of the television*

'It's nice to get out for a while': *It's nice to stand up for a change*

'The kids enjoyed it': *Fights and tears before bedtime*

'I'd better not, I'm driving': *I'd better not, I'm hungover*

'Did you get anything nice?': *Shame about the tie and cardigan*

'I must circulate': *I must escape*

'I'll be glad to get back to work': *At least there are no Ninja Turtles*

'We decided not to buy each other presents this year': *We thought we'd better pay the poll tax*

Ten things you'd love to do, but daren't

Say 'No' when the waiter asks if everything is all right

Tell the life-insurance man you're glad he phoned as you've just discovered that you only have six months to live

Ask the tattooed yob on the Tube to stop smoking

Switch over when the kids are watching *Top of the Pops*

Knock off the service from a restaurant bill where service is included

Tell the beggar to get a job and stop bothering people

Refuse to give when a charity collector rattles his box under your nose

Give a cab driver a 10p tip

Tell your neighbours to do something about the state of their garden

Say 'It's not enough' when the boss offers you a pay rise

Ten phrases to chill a parent's heart

'Can I borrow the car?'
'You know I borrowed the car last night . . .'
'Something's happened!'
'But everybody else has got one'
'This is your son's headmaster speaking'
'Can you have a look at my maths homework?'
'What's that man doing to that woman?'
'I feel si-ick!'
'Don't forget the school play on Saturday'
'But you promised'

Ten things which should be in everyone's bathroom cabinet

A rusting tin of Andrews Liver Salts
A half-empty bottle of cough syrup which is stuck
to the shelf
A worn-out emery board
A tube of indigestion tablets covered in talcum
powder
A plaster which is too big for any known cut
A complimentary bar of soap from a hotel
Last year's suntan lotion
Some tablets the doctor gave you years ago
A bottle of kaolin and morphine which has dripped
down the sides
A curled-up tube of antiseptic cream

Know your Highway Code – those road signs updated

 Rolling Stones concert ahead

 New Man zone

 You are approaching the Channel Tunnel

 Flying motorcycles

 Expect delays for up to two years

 Beware of ambush

 No entry for Luciano Pavarotti

 Tory Party Conference

 Pub car park ahead

 House prices forecast

BR-speak – a guide to interpretation

'Adverse weather conditions': *British climate*
'Modernisation programme': *Disruption for years to come*
'Staff shortages': *Driver has trouble getting out of bed in the morning*
'Incident on the line': *Cancellations finally got too much for one passenger*
'Maximum use of assets': *Standing room only*
'The train is late': *We've run out of excuses*
'Improvements': *Better TV commercials*
'Profit-oriented': *Inspectors now check tickets*
'Ninety per cent of trains arrive on time': *It's not our fault the public travels on the other 10 per cent*
'Travellers' Fare': *Sandwiches and cans of McEwan's Export*

The ten laws of DIY

'Handipaks' of screws always contain too few or
 too many for the job
Paint never looks the same on the wall as it does on
 the colour chart
Wallpaper is an animate object
If you have the right-sized washer, you have the
 wrong-sized spanner to unscrew the tap (and
 vice versa)
Swearing increases in inverse proportion to the
 amount of work completed
All jobs require at least one extra visit to the DIY
 centre
Few people ever fully recover from sanding
 wooden floors
There is no job so small that it can't be made
 longer by listening to advice
'Like putty in your hands' takes on a new and
 depressing meaning
The only easy part of wallpapering is lining
 drawers with the roll which is always left over

You know childhood is over when . . .

You don't automatically rush to the back seat
 when you get on a bus
You think book tokens are a good present to
 receive
You check your hair whenever you pass a mirror
You think fish fingers and baked beans are
 unsophisticated
You can spell unsophisticated
Someone calls you 'Sir' or 'Madam'
You start sunbathing
You choose your own clothes
You stop walking through puddles
You're embarrassed by your parents

The joys of parenthood –
ten things to look forward to

Tripping over Play People
Orange juice in the VCR
Trading in the sports car for a Volvo
Starting Christmas Day at three o'clock in the
 morning
Always eating at a Pizza Hut
Five in a bed on Saturday mornings
Pet burials
Being asked questions like 'What is earth?'
Not being able to get songs from Wally Whyton's
 Playtime out of your head
School plays

Ten things which should be in everyone's garden shed

Ten half-empty tins of solidified paint
A twisted wire coathanger for unblocking drains
Two boxes of bulbs dug up in 1975
A sun lounger with a ripped seat cover
A dozen cracked plastic seed trays
Two pairs of perished rubber gloves
Assorted car care products (unused)
Half a dozen spider webs
Two large cardboard boxes whose contents are unknown
Several paint brushes stuck in something crusty at the bottom of a jam jar

The thirtysomething generation – a guide to interpretation

Relationship: *Do you want to talk about it?*
Marriage: *The bringing together of two record collections*
Parents: *The dreaded sixtysomethings*
Free spirit: *Someone without a CD player*
Communicating: *Lots of hugging*
Moral crisis: *State or private education?*
Growing experience: *Separation*
Therapy: *Late-night chats over a bottle of Chardonnay*
Bruce Springsteen: *Said it all*
The future: *Fortysomething*

Ten visions of hell on earth

Being the only non-smoker at a dinner party
Having a bottle but no opener
Getting on the last bus with only a £20 note
Being asked to make an impromptu speech
Being coerced on stage by a hypnotist
Going to a talkative dentist
Being stuck on a desert island with eight Leonard Cohen records
Sitting next to a teething baby on a plane
Being unable to make the flush work at someone else's house
Being the only smoker at a dinner party

Advertising agency-speak – a guide to interpretation

'Concept': *What the rest of us call an idea*
'Minority interest': *TV programme which isn't introduced by Cilla Black*
'Typical housewife': *Worries about post-ironing smells*
'Shopping experience': *Shopping*
'Creative': *Wears large pink-framed glasses*
'Dynamic': *Someone who sacks all his staff*
'Nineties' man: *Carries baby around*
'Stylist': *Person who polishes tomatoes*
'Originality': *Using a 1950s pop song*
'Green consumer': *Licence to print money*

FILMS

Films for the faint-hearted

Conan the Librarian
Everything You Always Wanted to Know about
   Socks (But Were Afraid to Ask)
The Mild Bunch
The Texas Chainstore Massacre
Bob and Carol and Darby and Joan
Invasion of the Body Scratchers
Robochef
A Man Called Horace
9½ Leeks
Dial M for Maidstone

Oscar wild – ten Brits who won the Best Actor Academy Award

Charles Laughton (*The Private Life of Henry VIII*,
   1933)
Robert Donat (*Goodbye Mr Chips*, 1939)
Laurence Olivier (*Hamlet*, 1948)
Alec Guinness (*Bridge on the River Kwai*, 1957)
David Niven (*Separate Tables*, 1958)
Rex Harrison (*My Fair Lady*, 1964)
Paul Scofield (*A Man for All Seasons*, 1966)
Ben Kingsley (*Gandhi*, 1982)
Daniel Day Lewis (*My Left Foot*, 1990)
Jeremy Irons (*Reversal of Fortune*, 1991)

The ten unknown Marx Brothers

Garbo Marx: *the reclusive brother who was
   occasionally spotted in supermarkets*
Bronco Marx: *the sickly brother who was a martyr
   to diarrhoea all his life*
Rambo Marx: *the muscle-bound brother with a
   speech impediment*
Dumbo Marx: *the deaf-mute brother who taught
   Harpo all he knew*
Sumo Marx: *the incontinent brother who was
   forced to wear giant nappies*
Robbo Marx: *the sporting brother who was always
   injured*
Bimbo Marx: *the transvestite brother who was
   banned by the Hays Office*
Psycho Marx: *the wild-eyed brother with a shower
   fetish*
Sambo Marx: *the token non-white brother*
Brando Marx: *the brooding brother who always
   believed he could have been a contender*

Chico, Groucho and Harpo waiting for Psycho, Robbo
and Bimbo

Ten great wooden performances

The Log Lady's log in *Twin Peaks*
The vaulting horse in *The Wooden Horse*
Long John Silver's false leg in *Treasure Island*
The bridge in *The Bridge on the River Kwai*
The Trojan horse in *Helen of Troy*
The scenery in *Neighbours*
Sherwood Forest in *The Adventures of Robin Hood*
Al Capone's baseball bat in *The Untouchables*
The ship in *Mutiny on the Bounty*
The raft in *How the West was Won*

Ten films for the under-fives

The Pink Pamper
Infantasia
Ring of Gripe Water
High Chair Society
Postman Pat Always Rings Twice
Young Gums
I Was Monty's Dribble
Nightmare on Sesame Street
Prambo
The Creche from the Black Lagoon

Ten lines all actors learn at drama school

'One's so lucky to be paid for doing something one would do for nothing'
'Get the walk right and the rest of the character follows'
'Comedy's so much harder to do than the straight stuff'
'Of course, it always comes back to that playwright from Stratford'
'My ambition is just to keep working'
'Nothing matches live theatre for getting the adrenalin going'
'I was always mimicking the teachers at school, as a kind of defence mechanism I suppose'
'Awards are nice, but they're not what the business is all about'
'I think one learns to live with the insecurity – and be grateful for the times when one is in work'
'It may seem glamorous, but there's an awful lot of hanging around when you do film work'

Love according to the script

'Love means never having to say you're sorry' (Ryan O'Neal in *Love Story*)
'Love is like the measles – you only get it once and the older you are, the tougher it goes' (Howard Keel in *Seven Brides for Seven Brothers*)
'Love is a romantic designation for a most ordinary biological – or, shall we say, chemical – process' (Greta Garbo in *Ninotchka*)
'I love him because he's the kind of guy who gets drunk on buttermilk' (Barbara Stanwyck in *Ball of Fire*)
'Love is a miracle. It's like a birthmark – you can't hide it' (George Segal in *Blume in Love*)
'Maybe love is like luck – you have to go all the way to find it' (Robert Mitchum in *Out of the Past*)
'Send roses to room 424 and put "Emily, I love you" on the back of the bill' (Groucho Marx in *A Night in Casablanca*)
'Love is for the very young' (Kirk Douglas in *The Bad and the Beautiful*)
'You don't know what love means. To you, it's just another four-letter word' (Paul Newman in *Cat on a Hot Tin Roof*)
'Love isn't something you can put on or take off like an overcoat' (Arthur Kennedy in *Champion*)

Sounds like bull**** to me

Four down, four to go

Ten movie projects which might not make it into production

Mel Gibson in *Hamlet II*
Have I the Right, an Oliver Stone biopic of The Honeycombs' drummer
Three Men and an Old-Age Pensioner
Gérard Depardieu as Réné in a big screen version of *'Allo 'Allo*
The true story of the Celtic tribes, *Dances with Corgis*
Star Trek 12: The Search for Scotty's Waistline
A remake of *The Greatest Story Ever Told*, starring David Icke
Awakenings II, featuring the entire House of Lords
Silence of the Lambs – the Musical
Jason and Kylie in *The Tracy and Hepburn Story*

Green movies – ten films for gardeners

Back to the Fuchsia
101 Carnations
The Land that Thyme Forgot
Plantasia
The Cruel Seed
Butch Cassidy and the Sunflower Kid
A Fistful of Dahlias
The Magnificent Sedum
The Longest Daisy
The Germinator

Star-struck – ten couples who fell in love on film sets

Tom Cruise and Nicole Kidman (*Days of Thunder*)
Richard Burton and Elizabeth Taylor (*Cleopatra*)
William Hurt and Marlee Matlin (*Children of a Lesser God*)
Steve McQueen and Ali MacGraw (*The Getaway*)
Humphrey Bogart and Lauren Bacall (*To Have and Have Not*)
Spencer Tracy and Katharine Hepburn (*Woman of the Year*)
Nicolas Cage and Laura Dern (*Wild at Heart*)
John Malkovich and Michelle Pfeiffer (*Dangerous Liaisons*)
Warren Beatty and Madonna (*Dick Tracy*)
Kiefer Sutherland and Julia Roberts (*Flatliners*)

Identification? Certainly, officer

Ten movies for Oliver Reed to star in

Close Encounters of the Blurred Kind
For Whom the Bell's Tolls
The Booze Brothers
Billy Buddweiser
Romancing the Stone's
The Best Beers of Our Lives
The 39 Schnapps
My Brilliant Careering
Honey, I Drunk the Gins
Double Diamonds are Forever

Larger than life – ten actors who have played cartoon characters

Michael Keaton (Batman)
Robin Williams (Popeye)
Christopher Reeve (Superman)
Anouska Hempel (Tiffany Jones)
Lynda Carter (Wonder Woman)
Lou Ferrigno (The Incredible Hulk)
Warren Beatty (Dick Tracy)
Helen Slater (Supergirl)
Glynis Barber (Jane)
Monica Vitti (Modesty Blaise)

Always the bridesmaid never the bride: Oscar nominees who never won the glittering prize

Richard Burton (seven nominations)
Peter O'Toole (seven nominations)
Deborah Kerr (six nominations)
Alfred Hitchcock (five nominations)
Arthur Kennedy (five nominations)
Al Pacino (five nominations)
Mickey Rooney (four nominations)
Albert Finney (four nominations)
Marsha Mason (four nominations)
Glenn Close (four nominations)

Ten films you can grow in your garden

Goldfinger (Mexican sunflower)
African Queen (Lily)
Bright Eyes (Primula)
Summer Holiday (Rose)
Peter Pan (Zinnia)
Showboat (Marigold)
Paper Moon (Scabious)
Pinocchio (Aster)
Casablanca (Delphinium)
Cinderella (Snapdragon)

Ten lines you'd hear only in a Hollywood biopic

'You'll never finish that symphony the way you're going, Schubert'

'Can Benjamin come out kite flying, Mrs Franklin?'

'How many times do I have to tell you, Ludwig? Are you going deaf or something?'

'You must be mad if you think anyone's going to buy those, Vincent'

'Leave Stratford, Will, and make all the world your stage'

'Remember, Abe, you can't fool all of the people all of the time'

'How much longer are you going to be in that bathroom, Archimedes?'

'Come, comrade Marx, let's go gambling – we have nothing to lose but our change'

'Tonight, Napoleon?'

'George, what do you know about this cherry tree?'

'Action, dearest!' Ten men who have directed their wives in films

Mel Brooks (Anne Bancroft in *Silent Movie*)

Tony Richardson (Vanessa Redgrave in *The Charge of the Light Brigade*)

Orson Welles (Rita Hayworth in *The Lady from Shanghai*)

Bryan Forbes (Nanette Newman in *Seance on a Wet Afternoon*)

John Cassavetes (Gena Rowlands in *A Woman Under the Influence*)

Roman Polanski (Sharon Tate in *The Fearless Vampire Killers*)

Charlie Chaplin (Paulette Goddard in *Modern Times*)

Paul Newman (Joanne Woodward in *Rachel, Rachel*)

Vincente Minnelli (Judy Garland in *The Pirate*)

Anthony Newley (Joan Collins in *Can Hieronymus Merkin Ever Forget Mercy Humppe and Find True Happiness?*)

And I have one of Betty Grable's legs

Hot properties – ten items of film memorabilia sold at auction

Charlie Chaplin's hat and cane: £82,500 (Christie's 1987)

Charlie Chaplin's boots: £38,500 (Christie's 1987)

Marilyn Monroe's black satin dress from *Some Like It Hot*: £19,800 (Christie's 1988)

Model of Boris Karloff as Frankenstein's monster: £16,500 (Christie's 1988)

Giant boots worn by Elton John in *Tommy*: £12,100 (Sotheby's 1988)

Laurel and Hardy's hats: £11,000 (Christie's 1989)

Cape worn by Prince in *Purple Rain*: £7,150 (Sotheby's 1990)

Marilyn Monroe's black stiletto shoes from *Some Like It Hot*: £5,500 (Sotheby's 1989)

Promotional thermometer for *Some Like It Hot* featuring Marilyn Monroe down the centre: £5,060 (Phillips 1989)

A pair of black suede stiletto shoes worn by Marilyn Monroe in *Let's Make Love*: £3,520 (Phillips 1990)

Ten movie sequels we're waiting for

Willy Wonka and the Dental Appointment

The Postgraduate

Babette's Washing-Up

Saturday the 14th

The Retirement of Duddy Kravitz

Total Memory Loss

Three Men and a Teenager

Sunday Night and Monday Morning

Conditioner

The Postman always pushes a Card through the Door asking you to go down to the Sorting Office

Did he shoot six movies, or was it only five?

If at first you don't succeed . . . Clint Eastwood's first ten movies

Revenge of the Creature (1955)
Francis in the Navy (1955)
Lady Godiva (1955)
Tarantula! (1956)
Never Say Goodbye (1956)
Star in the Dust (1956)
The First Travelling Saleslady (1956)
Escapade in Japan (1957)
Lafayette Escadrille (1957)
Ambush at Cimarron Pass (1958)
(No 11 was *A Fistful of Dollars* in 1964)

The ten greatest disaster movies (financially, that is)

The Adventures of Baron Munchausen (1988): lost $48.1m
Ishtar (1987): lost $47.3m
Inchon (1981): lost $44.1m
The Cotton Club (1984): lost $38.1m
Santa Claus: The Movie (1985): lost $37m
Heaven's Gate (1980): lost $34.2m
Pirates (1986): lost $30.3m
Rambo III (1988): lost $30m
Raise The Titanic (1980): lost $29.2m
Revolution (1985): lost $27m

The first ten movies to win the Best Film Oscar

Wings (1928)
Broadway Melody (1929)
All Quiet on the Western Front (1930)
Cimarron (1931)
Grand Hotel (1932)
Cavalcade (1933)
It Happened One Night (1934)
Mutiny on the Bounty (1935)
The Great Ziegfeld (1936)
The Life of Emile Zola (1937)

The pervert's film guide

Full Rubber Jacket
Bob and Carol and Ted and Fido
The Thong of Norway
Gentlemen Prefer Bonds
Those Magnificent Men in Their Flaying Machines
The Man Who Would Be Queen
The Dirty Dozen Raincoats
The John Thomas Crown Affair
Goodbye, Mr Whips
The Man in the Iron Basque

How Bergmanesque!
A guide to serious film crits

'An erotic comedy of manners': *Socially acceptable skinflick*

'Loosely-woven narrative structure': *No plot*

'Ends on an enigmatic note': *Impossible to work out who did it*

'Full of raw energy': *They didn't edit it*

'Imbued with moral uncertainties': *Hero sleeps with all the women*

'Notable for its chromatic dichotomy': *Bits are in black and white*

'Self-referential': *Rambo XII*

'Recently reappraised': *You can now admit to liking it*

'Cinéma vérité': *Shaky camera*

'Confirms the emergence of Third World cinema': *Subtitled*

Ten actresses who have played hookers (happy or otherwise)

Shirley Maclaine (*Irma la Douce*)
Sophia Loren (*Lady L*)
Carroll Baker (*Sylvia*)
Nancy Kwan (*The World of Suzie Wong*)
Melina Mercouri (*Never on a Sunday*)
Jane Fonda (*Klute*)
Julia Roberts (*Pretty Woman*)
Catherine Deneuve (*Belle de Jour*)
Diane Cilento (*Rattle of a Simple Man*)
Carol White (*Poor Cow*)

Ten movies for a recession

Debt in Venice
The King and IOU
Penny from Heaven
The Loan Arranger
Begging Letter to Brezhnev
The Owed Curiosity Shop
A Comedy of Arrears
Hock around the Clock
Bill de Jour
This Gun for Hire Purchase

A 1–10 of Oscar-winning films

Klute (1)
Aliens (2)
A Room with a View (3)
Platoon (4)
Who's Afraid of Virginia Woolf? (5)
The Godfather Part II (6)
Out of Africa (7)
Gandhi (8)
The Last Emperor (9)
West Side Story (10)

Julia Roberts: a game girl?

The first ten winners of the Best Actress Oscar

Janet Gaynor (*Seventh Heaven*, 1928)
Mary Pickford (*Coquette*, 1929)
Norma Shearer (*The Divorcee*, 1930)
Marie Dressler (*Min and Bill*, 1931)
Helen Hayes (*Sin of Madelon Claudet*, 1932)
Katharine Hepburn (*Morning Glory*, 1933)
Claudette Colbert (*It Happened One Night*, 1934)
Bette Davis (*Dangerous*, 1935)
Luise Rainer (*The Great Ziegfeld*, 1936)
Luise Rainer (*The Good Earth*, 1937)

The first ten winners of the Best Actor Oscar

Emil Jannings (*The Last Command*, 1928)
Warner Baxter (*In Old Arizona*, 1929)
George Arliss (*Disraeli*, 1930)
Lionel Barrymore (*A Free Soul*, 1931)
Fredric March (*Dr Jekyll and Mr Hyde*) and
   Wallace Beery (*The Champ*, 1932)
Charles Laughton (*The Private Life of Henry VIII*,
   1933)
Clark Gable (*It Happened One Night*, 1934)
Victor McLaglen (*The Informer*, 1935)
Paul Muni (*The Story of Louis Pasteur*, 1936)
Spencer Tracy (*Captains Courageous*, 1937)

Ten films for royal premieres

The Man who Fell to Earth (Prince Charles)
Charley's Aunt (Princess Margaret)
Outrageous Fortune (The Queen)
Rancho Deluxe (The Duke of York)
Bringing up Baby (The Duchess of York)
The Trouble with Harry (Prince William)
The Good Companions (The Princess Royal and
   Timothy Laurence)
It's a Wonderful Life (The Queen Mother)
The Prince and the Pauper (Prince Michael of
   Kent)
The Wild One (Prince Edward)

It's a wrap – ten memorable last lines of movies

'Louis, I think this is the beginning of a beautiful
   friendship' (Humphrey Bogart in *Casablanca*)
'Look, Ma, top of the world' (James Cagney in
   White Heat)
'Marry me, Emily, and I'll never look at any other
   horse' (Groucho Marx in *A Day at the Races*)
'Oh, Jerry, don't let's ask for the moon, we have
   the stars' (Bette Davis in *Now Voyager*)
'Tomorrow is another day' (Vivien Leigh in *Gone
   With the Wind*)
'Good, for a minute I thought we were in trouble'
   (Paul Newman in *Butch Cassidy and the
   Sundance Kid*)
'Oh, Aunt Em, there's no place like home' (Judy
   Garland in *The Wizard of Oz*)
'All right, Mr De Mille, I'm ready for my close-up'
   (Gloria Swanson in *Sunset Boulevard*)
'I now pronounce you men and wives' (Ian Wolfe
   in *Seven Brides for Seven Brothers*)
'The lobsters are back!' (Michael Craig in *High
   Tide at Noon*)

Unlucky in love, lucky in friendship

Cricket commentator-speak – a guide to interpretation

'This young man has caught the eye of the England selectors': *Often reaches double figures*

'He's always prepared to try something new': *You don't often see the wicket-keeper bowling*

'That must have been very close': *He was out*

'He's certainly got the batsmen puzzled': *He hasn't got a ball on the wicket in the last three overs*

'He has a tendency to sacrifice accuracy for that extra bit of pace': *Another wide*

'The batsmen should be in no danger here': *Tea interval*

'My old mother could've caught that in 'er pinny': *Expert analysis by Geoff Boycott*

'Unorthodox, but effective': *Ball bounced off the batsman's helmet and went for six*

'There's a couple of bouncers that shouldn't trouble the batsmen': *Weak joke about a streaker*

'Let's have a look at some highlights from the last series': *Rain stops play*

Ten commandments for footballers

Thou shalt not take the name of the referee in vain within his hearing

Thou shalt not steal ten yards in a free kick situation

Thou shalt not bear false witness against the opposition's No. 5 to get him sent off

Thou shalt honour thy manager, thy trainer and the terms of thy contract

Thou shalt train for five days and on the sixth 'go out and do the business'

Thou shalt turn up for extra training on the seventh day if thou hast failed to do the business on the sixth

Thou shalt have no other gods before the one true god known as Work Rate

Thou shalt speak to nobody without first getting an agent

Thou shalt not indulge in off-the-ball incidents if the TV cameras are there

Thou shalt not covet thy club captain's sponsored Vauxhall Senator

So you're a soccer star? Ten tell-tale signs

Brian Clough calls you 'The boy Smith'
Jimmy Greaves calls you 'Smiffy'
The tabloids call you 'Smazza'
You discover you've written an autobiography
Your first girlfriend sells her story to the *News of the World*
Your old headmaster appears on *Wogan*
Jimmy Hill analyses your work rate
The Italians make you an offer you can't understand
You are invited round to No. 10 for a 'Prop up the PM' photo-call
You keep finding blonde stowaways in your underwear

All in the family – a fathers v sons cricket match

Alan Butcher (Glamorgan): Mark Butcher (Surrey)
Les Lenham (Sussex): Neil Lenham (Sussex)
David Lloyd (Lancashire): Graham Lloyd (Lancashire)
Donald Carr (Derbyshire): John Carr (Middlesex)
Mike Smith (Warwickshire): Neil Smith (Warwickshire)
Colin Cowdrey (Kent): Chris Cowdrey (Kent)
Basil D'Oliveira (Worcestershire): Damian D'Oliveira (Worcestershire)
Micky Stewart (Surrey): Alec Stewart (Surrey)
Jim Parks (Sussex): Bobby Parks (Hampshire)
Ken Graveney (Gloucestershire): David Graveney (Somerset)
John Wild (Northamptonshire): Duncan Wild (Northamptonshire)

Ten things we expect Gazza to do in 1992

Make a guest appearance in *The Darling Buds of May*
Bring out 'Gazza's Guide to Geordie Cooking'
Record an album with Nigel Kennedy
Be photographed with his arm around George Bush
Be photographed with his arm around the Pope
Find a decent hairdresser
Star opposite Sylvester Stallone in *Rocky VI*
Sing at the Royal Variety Show
Appear on *The Best of Morecambe & Wise*
Learn to tackle properly

Ten unsporting quotes

'If Everton were playing down at the bottom of my garden, I'd draw the curtains' (Bill Shankly)

'It's hard playing against a man' (Hana Mandlikova on Martina Navratilova)

'You're very deceptive, son, you're even slower than you look' (Tommy Docherty on Leighton James)

'Ted Dexter is to journalism what Danny La Rue is to rugby league' (Michael Parkinson)

'Frazier is so ugly he should donate his face to the US Bureau of Wildlife' (Muhammad Ali)

'The only time our girls looked good at the Munich Olympics was in the village discotheque between nine and eleven every night' (US coach)

'He has done as much for the image of our sport as Cyril Smith would do for hang-gliding' (Reg Bowden on Eddie Waring)

'Billie Jean King's father put her into tennis to stop her being a woman wrestler' (Jim Murray)

'I thought he was one of the human race – but he is not' (Alain Prost on Ayrton Senna)

'I've seen him shadow boxing and the shadow won' (Muhammad Ali on George Foreman)

Stinging like a bee

Home and away – a Football League XI born abroad

Bruce Grobbelaar, Liverpool (South Africa)
Gudni Bergsson, Tottenham Hotspur (Iceland)
Tony Dorigo, Leeds United (Australia)
Detsi Kruszynski, Wimbledon (Poland)
Terry Butcher, Coventry City (Singapore)
Kenneth Monkou, Chelsea (Surinam)
Anders Limpar, Arsenal (Sweden)
Nayim, Tottenham Hotspur (Morocco)
Cyrille Regis, Aston Villa (French Guyana)
John Barnes, Liverpool (Jamaica)
Ronny Rosenthal, Liverpool (Israel)

Match of the Day – fathers v sons

Roy Bailey (Ipswich): Gary Bailey (Manchester United)
John Bond (West Ham): Kevin Bond (Bournemouth)
Ian Bowyer (Nottingham Forest): Gary Bowyer (Nottingham Forest)
George Wilkins (Brentford): Ray Wilkins (QPR)
John Aston (Manchester United): John Aston (Manchester United)
Doug Webb (Reading): Neil Webb (Manchester United)
Harry Redknapp (West Ham): Jamie Redknapp (Liverpool)
George Eastham (Blackpool): George Eastham (Arsenal)
Brian Clough (Middlesborough): Nigel Clough (Nottingham Forest)
Tony Hateley (Aston Villa): Mark Hateley (Rangers)
Ken Barnes (Manchester City): Peter Barnes (Manchester City)

Title winners – ten titles of football fanzines

Mission Impossible (Torquay United)
Liverpool Are On The Tele Again! (Norwich City)
Waiting For The Great Leap Forward (Motherwell)
The Memoirs Of Seth Bottomley (Port Vale)
Shots In The Dark (Aldershot)
Dial M For Merthyr (Merthyr Tydfil)
The 92nd Club (Rochdale)
Brian Moore's Head Looks Uncannily Like The London Planetarium (Gillingham)
A Load Of Bull (Wolves)
Friday Night Fever (Tranmere Rovers)

Test Match Special – the British Academy of Cricket Television Awards

Best coverage of rain stopped play

Best Viv Richards interview (non-violent category)

The Fred Trueman 'I just don't understand it' Award for something Fred just doesn't understand

Moodiest stare at an umpire after a dubious lbw decision

Most unorthodox catch requiring hospital treatment

Most frequent use of the phrase 'line and length' by a commentator

Most vigorous adjustment of box

Most tasteful coverage of a streaker

Most humorous dog-on-pitch interlude

Best coverage of tea interval

An England Cricket XI of England cricket captains

Graham Gooch (Essex)
Mike Brearley (Middlesex)
Colin Cowdrey (Kent)
Ted Dexter (Sussex)
David Gower (Hampshire)
Ian Botham (Somerset/Worcestershire)
Tony Greig (Sussex)
Ray Illingworth (Leicestershire)
R T Stanyforth, wicketkeeper (Yorkshire)
John Emburey (Middlesex)
Bob Willis (Warwickshire)

A foodie football team

Steve Pears (Middlesbrough)
Paul Bacon (Charlton)
Neil Berry (Hearts)
Peter Haddock (Leeds)
Jesse Roast (Maidstone)
Barry Venison (Liverpool)
Brian Rice (Nottingham Forest)
Nigel Pepper (York)
Michael Mellon (Bristol City)
Frankie Bunn (Oldham)
Chris Fry (Hereford United)

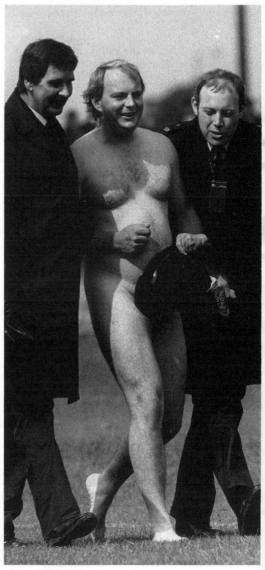

Well caught, officer

Kevin's taking it on the chin . . .

. . . while George ties one on

Kick them where it hurts – ten quotes about footballers

Trevor Brooking: 'Trevor Brooking floats like a butterfly and stings like one too' (Brian Clough)

Ray Wilkins: 'The only time he goes forward is to toss the coin' (Tommy Docherty)

Paul Gascoigne: 'George Best without brains' (Stan Seymour)

Glenn Hoddle: 'You can scare Hoddle out of a match and you couldn't depend on him to bring you a cup of tea if you were dying' (Tommy Smith)

Stan Bowles: 'If Stan could pass a betting shop like he can pass a ball, he'd have no worries at all' (Ernie Tagg)

Kevin Keegan: 'He's not fit to lace my boots as a player' (George Best)

Kevin Keegan: 'Keegan is not fit to lace George Best's drinks' (John Roberts)

Martin Peters: 'He's the one who's ten years ahead of his time, so we've got to wait for him to come good' (Malcolm Allison)

Kenny Dalglish: 'Kenny Dalglish has about as much personality as a tennis racket' (Mike Channon)

John Fashanu: 'He couldn't hit a cow's arse with a banjo' (Dave Bassett)

Ten events for the Atlanta Olympics

Gator wrasslin'
Hog callin'
Whistlin' Dixie
Totin' dat bale
Shufflin' down de levee
Liftin' dat barge
Kickin' yo' butt
Marchin' thru Georgia
Waitin' for de Robert E Lee
Burnin' cross-country run

The ten ages of a soccer star

Described as a 'talented newcomer with all the skills'

Acquires a 1970s hairstyle

Described as 'talented, but wayward'

Acquires a nickname and an agent

Signed up to write a ghosted newspaper column

Moves to a Continental club 'to make my family financially secure'

Moves back 'because my wife was homesick'

Becomes player-manager of a Second Division club and takes them into the Third

Receives a 'vote of confidence' from the board – and is dismissed shortly afterwards

Acquires a 1980s hairstyle and becomes a TV pundit

QUOTATIONS

Sleeping with the enemy – ten quotes about marriage

'Marriage is a good deal like taking a hot bath – not so hot once you get used to it' (Bill Lawrence)

'When a girl marries, she exchanges the attentions of many men for the inattention of one' (Helen Rowland)

'All marriages are happy – it's the living together afterwards that causes all the trouble' (Raymond Hull)

'Marriage is a triumph of habit over hate' (Oscar Levant)

'The most labour-saving device today is still a husband with money' (Joey Adams)

'Marriage is a lot like the army – everyone complains but you'd be surprised at the large number that re-enlist (James Garner)

'Marriage is a romance in which the hero dies in the first chapter' (J.P. McEvoy)

'Marriage is based on the theory that when a man discovers a brand of beer to his taste, he should at once throw up his job and go to work in the brewery' (George Nathan)

'When a man brings his wife flowers for no reason – there's a reason' (Molly McGee)

'Marriage demands the greatest understanding of the art of insincerity possible between two human beings' (Vicki Baum)

Going Zsa Zsa – ten quotes from Ms Gabor

'You never really know a man until you've divorced him'

'I want a man who's kind and understanding – is that too much to ask of a millionaire?'

'I believe in large families: every woman should have at least three husbands'

'I never really hated a man enough to give him his diamonds back'

'I'm a marvellous housekeeper – every time I leave a man I keep his house'

'Getting divorced just because you don't love a man is almost as silly as getting married just because you love him'

'The only place men want depth in a woman is in her *décolletage*'

'The women's movement hasn't changed my sex life at all: it wouldn't dare'

'If they had as much adultery going on in New York as they said in the divorce courts, they would never have a chance to make the beds at the Plaza'

'You mean apart from my own?' (when asked how many husbands she'd had)

The world's greatest housekeeper, Darlink

. . . keeping the White House free from whitewash

Ten presidential put-downs

Gerry Ford is a nice guy, but he played too much football with his helmet off' (Lyndon Johnson)

Washington could not tell a lie; Nixon could not tell the truth; Reagan cannot tell the difference' (Mort Sahl)

I would not want Jimmy Carter and his men put in charge of snake control in Ireland' (Eugene McCarthy)

Lyndon Johnson's strategy is too slick to talk about and so subtle that only a few fellow con men appreciate it' (I F Stone)

Do you realise the responsibility I carry? I'm the only person standing between Richard Nixon and the White House' (John F Kennedy)

If I talk over people's heads, Ike must talk under their feet' (Adlai Stevenson on Dwight D Eisenhower)

How can they tell?' (Dorothy Parker on being told that Calvin Coolidge was dead)

We've got the kind of president who thinks arms control means some kind of deodorant' (Pat Schroeder on Ronald Reagan)

Gerald Ford was unknown throughout America. Now he's unknown throughout the world' (Anon)

He told us he was going to take crime out of the streets. He did. He took it into the damn White House' (Ralph Abernathy on Richard Nixon)

Ten catty remarks

'A cat will dole out just enough affection to ensure a continuing supply of food' (Joshua Thomas)

'Cats are irresponsible and recognise no authority, yet are completely dependent on others for their material needs' (P J O'Rourke)

'Cats, like men, are flatterers' (Walter Savage Landor)

'If a dog jumps on to your lap it is because he is fond of you, but if a cat does the same thing it is because your lap is warmer' (A N Whitehead)

'The trouble with a kitten is that eventually it becomes a cat' (Ogden Nash)

'Cats seem to go on the principle that it never does any harm to ask for what you want' (Joseph Wood Krutch)

'People with insufficient personalities are fond of cats – such people adore being ignored' (Henry Morgan)

'When I play with my cat, who knows whether she is not amusing herself more with me than I with her?' (Michel de Montaigne)

'A dog . . . wants to please everybody – a cat really doesn't need to know that everybody loves him' (William Kunstler)

'What cats most appreciate in a human being is not the ability to produce food, which they take for granted, but his or her entertainment value' . (Geoffrey Household)

You can't fool all the people all the time – ten thoughts on advertising

'Advertising is legalised lying' (H G Wells)

'Advertising may be described as the science of arresting human intelligence long enough to get money from it' (Stephen Leacock)

'You can tell the ideals of a nation by its advertisements' (Norman Douglas)

'In good times people want to advertise, in bad times they have to' (Bruce Barton)

'Ads are the cave art of the twentieth century' (Marshall McLuhan)

'Advertising is the rattling of a stick inside a swill bucket' (George Orwell)

'Advertising is the art of making whole lies out of half truths' (Edgar Shoaff)

'Doing business without advertising is like winking at a girl in the dark – you know what you are doing, but nobody else does' (Stuart Henderson Britt)

'Research men in advertising are really blind men groping in a dark room for a black cat that isn't there' (Ludovic Kennedy)

'Advertising is the whip which hustles humanity up the road to the better mousetrap' (E S Turner)

It's a dog-owner's life – ten quotes about man's best friend

'To his dog, every man is Napoleon, hence the constant popularity of dogs' (Aldous Huxley)

'A dog teaches a boy fidelity, perseverance and to turn round three times before lying down' (Robert Benchley)

'Anybody who hates children and dogs can't be all bad' (W C Fields)

'The greatest pleasure of a dog is that you may make a fool of yourself with him and not only will he not scold you, he will make a fool of himself too' (Samuel Butler)

'The woman who is really kind to dogs is always one who has failed to inspire sympathy in men' (Max Beerbohm)

'I loathe people who keep dogs – they are cowards who haven't got the guts to bite people themselves' (August Strindberg)

'A dog is the only thing on Earth that loves you more than you love yourself' (Josh Billings)

'That indefatigable and unsavoury engine of pollution, the dog' (John Sparrow)

'The censure of a dog is something no man can stand' (Christopher Morley)

'When a dog bites a man that is not news, but when a man bits a dog that is news' (Charles Anderson Dana)

Ten quotes about power

'If absolute power corrupts absolutely, where does that leave God?' (George Dacon)

'A friend in power is a friend lost' (Henry Adams)

'Power is the ultimate aphrodisiac' (Henry Kissinger)

'Being powerful is like being a lady – if you have to tell people you are, you ain't' (Jesse Carr)

'The men who really wield, retain and covet power are the kind who answer bedside telephones while making love' (Nicholas Pileggi)

'When a man is intoxicated by alcohol he can recover, but when intoxicated by power he seldom recovers' (James Byrne)

'People rise to a level of power just one step beneath that which would make them feel secure' (Michael Korda)

'The wrong sort of people are always in power, because they would not be in power if they were not the wrong sort of people' (Jon Wynne Tyson)

'Power only tires those who don't exercise it' (Pierre Trudeau)

'The problem of power is how to get men of power to live for the public rather than off the public' (Robert Kennedy)

Many happy returns – ten quotes about taxation

'In this world nothing is certain but death and taxes' (Benjamin Franklin)

'The taxpayer is someone who works for the federal government but doesn't have to take a civil service examination' (Ronald Reagan)

'The income tax people are very nice – they're letting me keep my own mother' (Henny Youngman)

'The hardest thing in the world to understand is income tax' (Albert Einstein)

'Taxation without representation is tyranny' (James Otis)

'The income tax has made more liars out of the American people than golf has' (Will Rogers)

'There is no art which one government sooner learns of another than that of draining money from the pockets of the people' (Adam Smith)

'Income tax returns are the most imaginative fiction being written today' (Herman Wouk)

'The avoidance of taxes is the only pursuit that still carries any reward' (John Maynard Keynes)

'I believe we should all pay our tax bill with a smile. I tried – but they wanted cash' (Anon)

Albert: only relatively bemused

In memoriam – ten notable last words

'Either that wallpaper goes or I do' (Oscar Wilde)

'That was a great game of golf, fellas' (Bing Crosby)

'Doctor, do you think it could have been the sausage?' (Paul Claudel)

'Go away, I'm alright' (H G Wells)

'If this is dying, I don't think much of it' (Lytton Strachey)

'I should never have switched from Scotch to Martinis' (Humphrey Bogart)

'Come, come – why, they couldn't hit an elephant at this dist . . .' (John Sedgwick, American Civil War general)

'Die, my doctor, that's the last thing I shall do!' (Lord Palmerston)

'I have a terrific headache' (Franklin D Roosevelt)

'How were the receipts today in Madison Square Garden?' (P T Barnum)

We shouldn't really be telling you this, but . . . ten quotes about gossip

'Gossip is when you hear something you like about someone you don't like' (Earl Wilson)

'Gossip is the art of saying nothing in a way that leaves practically nothing unsaid' (Walter Winchell)

'No one gossips about other people's secret virtues' (Bertrand Russell)

'A gossip is a person with a keen sense of rumour' (Eleanor Doan)

'Hating anything in the way of ill-natured gossip ourselves, we are always grateful to those who do it for us and do it well' (Saki)

'There is only one thing in the world worse than being talked about, and that is not being talked about' (Oscar Wilde)

'A good gossip is a wonderful tonic' (The Queen)

'She always tells stories in the present vindictive' (Tom Pearce)

'There are many who dare not kill themselves for fear of what the neighbours will say' (Cyril Connolly)

'When gossip grows old it becomes myth' (Stanislaw Lec)

We do enjoy a tonic

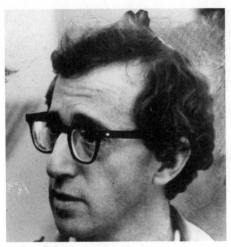
Waiting for pennies from heaven

God only knows –
ten quotes about religion

'If only God would give me some clear sign – like making a large deposit in my name in a Swiss bank' (Woody Allen)

'God is dead, but 50,000 social workers have risen to take His place' (Dr J D McCoughey)

'God seems to have left the receiver off the hook and time is running out' (Arthur Koestler)

'In the beginning was the word – it's about the only sentence on which I find myself in total agreement with God' (John Mortimer)

'Religion is the tendency to prefer God to the government, most commonly found in Communist countries' (Miles Kington)

'The English are probably the most tolerant, least religious people on earth' (Rabbi David Goldberg)

'I do benefits for all religions – I'd hate to blow the hereafter on a technicality' (Bob Hope)

'A cult is a religion with no political power' (Tom Wolfe)

'Jesus Christ was not a Conservative, that's a racing certainty' (Eric Heffer)

'God is alive – he just doesn't want to get involved' (Anon)

By George – ten George Burns quotes

'I can remember when the air was clean and sex was dirty'

'When I was a young man, the Dead Sea was still alive'

'Whenever I complain that things aren't what they used to be, I always forget to include myself'

'I have my eighty-seventh birthday coming up and people ask what I'd most appreciate getting. I'll tell you: a paternity suit'

'With the collapse of vaudeville new talent has no place to stink'

'I smoke ten to fifteen cigars a day – at my age I have to hold on to something'

'Acting is all about honesty. If you can fake that, you've got it made'

'Too bad all the people who know how to run the country are busy driving taxi cabs and cutting hair'

'Retirement at sixty-five is ridiculous. When I was sixty-five I still had pimples'

'Actually, it only takes one drink to get me loaded. Trouble is I can't remember if it's the thirteenth or fourteenth'

Class consciousness –
ten quotes about school

'Headmasters have powers at their disposal with which prime ministers have never yet been invested' (Sir Winston Churchill)

'I have never let my schooling interfere with my education' (Mark Twain)

'In real life, I assure you, there is no such thing as algebra' (Fran Lebowitz)

'If every day in the life of a school could be the last day but one, there would be little fault to find with it' (Stephen Leacock)

'A man who has never gone to school may steal from a freight car – if he has a university education, he may steal the whole railroad' (Theodore Roosevelt)

'Anyone who has been to an English public school will always feel comparatively at home in prison' (Evelyn Waugh)

'No one who had any sense has ever liked school' (Lord Boothby)

'Show me a man who had enjoyed his schooldays and I'll show you a bully and a bore' (Robert Morley)

'School is where you go between when your parents can't take you and industry can't take you' (John Updike)

'A public schoolboy must be acceptable at a dance and invaluable in a shipwreck' (Alan Bennett)

A cynic writes –
Oscar Wilde on relationships

The proper basis for marriage is a mutual misunderstanding'

'The one charm of marriage is that it makes a life of deception absolutely necessary for both parties'

'No man should have a secret from his wife; she invariably finds it out'

'There's nothing in the world like the devotion of a married woman; it's the thing no married man knows anything about'

'One can always recognise women who trust their husbands; they look so thoroughly unhappy'

'Modern women understand everything except their husbands'

'Men marry because they are tired, women because they are curious; both are disappointed'

'One should always be in love; that is the reason one should never marry'

'A man can be happy with any woman as long as he does not love her'

'The Book of Life begins with a man and a woman in a garden, and it ends with Revelations'

No, prime minister

The art of the possible –
ten quotes about politics

'A politician is a statesman who approaches every question with an open mouth' (Adlai Stevenson)

'It rarely pays in politics to be wise before the event' (Chris Patten)

'Now I know what a statesman is: he's a dead politician' (Bob Edwards)

'Nothing is so admirable in politics as a short memory' (J K Galbraith)

'Politicians are the same all over – they promise to build a bridge even where there's no river' (Nikita Khrushchev)

'I always wanted to get into politics, but I was never light enough to get in the team' (Art Buchwald)

'Politics: the gentle art of getting votes from the poor and campaign funds from the rich by promising to protect each from the other' (Oscar Ameringer)

'The connection between humbug and politics is too long established to be challenged' (Ronald Bell)

'All politics are best on the indifference of the majority' (James Reston)

'Politics is a blood sport' (Aneurin Bevan)

How wrong can you be?
Ten cases of foot-in-mouth disease

'Ayatollah Khomeini will one day be viewed as some kind of a saint' (Andrew Young, 1976)

'In all likelihood, world inflation is over' (Per Jacobsson, Director of the IMF, 1959)

'Read my lips – no new taxes' (George Bush, 1988)

'No woman in my time will be Prime Minister or Foreign Secretary, not the top jobs – anyway, I wouldn't want to be Prime Minister' (Margaret Thatcher, 1969)

'Iran is an island of stability in one of the most volatile parts of the world' (Jimmy Carter, 1977)

'Anyone who looks for a source of power in the transformation of the atom is talking moonshine' (Sir Ernest Rutherford, 1933)

'Let us begin by committing ourselves to the truth, to see it like it is and to tell it like it is, to find the truth, to speak the truth and to live with the truth' (Richard Nixon, 1968)

'This picture is going to be one of the biggest white elephants of all time' (Victor Fleming, director of *Gone with the Wind*, 1939)

'We believe that a centre party would have no roots, no principles, no philosophy and no values' (Shirley Williams, 1980)

'We will make them grovel' (Tony Greig before losing a Test series 3–0 to the West Indies, 1976)

Get to know our European neighbours – ten quotes for 1992

'The problem with Ireland is that it's a country full of genius, but with absolutely no talent' (Hugh Leonard)

'German is the most extravagantly ugly language – it sounds like someone using a sick bag on a 747' (Willie Rushton)

'France is a country where the money falls apart and you can't tear the toilet paper' (Billy Wilder)

'From Hamlet to Kierkegaard, the word "Danish" has been synonymous with fun, fun, fun' (Tony Hendra)

'It is not impossible to govern the Italians, it is merely useless' (Benito Mussolini)

'Spain – a country that has sold its soul for cement and petrol and can only be saved by a series of earthquakes' (Cyril Connolly)

'If there is no Portuguese word for blarney, there should be' (Richard West)

'The Greeks – impoverished descendants of a bunch of la-de-da fruit salads who invented democracy and then forgot how to use it while walking around dressed up like girls' (P J O'Rourke)

'A Belgian is a hell living on earth' (Charles Baudelaire)

'Continental people have sex lives – the English have hot-water bottles' (George Mikes)

The world according to H L Mencken

'Love is the delusion that one woman differs from another'

'Bachelors know more about women than married men; if they didn't, they'd be married too'

'A gentleman is one who never strikes a woman without provocation'

'On one issue at least, men and women agree: they both distrust women'

'Conscience is the inner voice that warns us that someone may be looking'

'It is a sin to believe evil of others, but it is seldom a mistake'

'Puritanism: the haunting fear that someone, somewhere, may be happy'

'Self-respect: the secure feeling that no one, as yet, is suspicious'

'A cynic is a man who, when he smells flowers, looks around for a coffin'

'A politician is an animal that can sit on a fence and keep both ears to the ground'

MUSIC

Joining the popocracy – ten signs that you've made it as a rock star

You play cricket with Tim, soccer with Rod and
    tennis with Cliff
Simon Bates refers to you as 'My good friend'
Mark Knopfler plays guitar on your latest album
You are served with a paternity suit
The *NME* dismisses you as a 'dinosaur'
You are recognised even when wearing your Ray-
    Bans
You organise a charity event to save the planet
Bob Dylan asks you to play on his next album
Flight attendants provide your favourite Marmite
    sandwiches when you travel on Concorde
You record a protest song against world poverty at
    the studios on your Caribbean island

A big hit for little Jimmy

Stars over 45 – the ten oldest chart-toppers

Louis Armstrong, aged 69: *What a Wonderful
    World* (1968)
Clive Dunn, aged 52: *Grandad* (1970)
Frank Sinatra, aged 51: *Somethin' Stupid* (with
    Nancy Sinatra, 1967)
Cliff Richard, aged 50: *Saviour's Day* (1990)
Charles Aznavour, aged 50: *She* (1974)
Telly Savalas, aged 50: *If* (1975)
Ben E. King, aged 49: *Stand by Me* (1987)
Gene Pitney, aged 48: *Something's Gotten Hold of
    My Heart*, (with Marc Almond, 1989)
Mantovani, aged 47: *Moulin Rouge* (1953)
Benny Hill, aged 46: *Ernie* (1971)

Top of the tots – the ten youngest singers to make the Top Ten

Little Jimmy Osmond, aged 9 (*Long Haired Lover
    from Liverpool*, 1972)
Lena Zavaroni, aged 10 (*Ma He's Making Eyes at
    Me*, 1974)
Michael Jackson as part of the Jackson Five, aged
    11 (*I Want You Back*, 1970)
Neil Reid, aged 12 (*Mother of Mine*, 1972)
Ralph Tresvant as part of New Edition, aged 13
    (*Candy Girl*, 1983)
Frankie Lymon, aged 13 (*Why do Fools Fall in
    Love*, 1956)
Helen Shapiro, aged 14 (*Don't Treat Me like a
    Child*, 1961)
Dennis Seaton as part of Musical Youth, aged 14
    (*Pass the Dutchie*, 1982)
Aled Jones, aged 14 (*Walking in the Air*, 1985)
Lulu, aged 15 (*Shout*, 1964)

Strangled in the night –
the top ten karaoke songs

My Way
Summer Nights
New York, New York
Fame
It's not Unusual
You've Lost that Lovin' Feelin'
La Bamba
Addicted to Love
Girls Just Wanna Have Fun
I Will Survive

After the book . . . the pop song

1984 (George Orwell/Eurythmics)
The Cruel Sea (Nicholas Monsarrat/The Dakotas)
Wuthering Heights (Emily Brontë/Kate Bush)
Lust for Life (Irving Stone/Iggy Pop)
Bleak House (Charles Dickens/Nero & The Gladiators)
Dogs of War (Frederick Forsyth/Pink Floyd)
Romeo and Juliet (William Shakespeare/Dire Straits)
The Loneliness of the Long Distance Runner (Alan Sillitoe/Iron Maiden)
Live and Let Die (Ian Fleming/Paul McCartney)
Torch Song (Jack Kerouac/Marillion)

Songs for swinging livers

Whisky in the Jar (Thin Lizzy)
Brandy (Scott English)
Sherry (Adrian Baker)
Gin House (Amen Corner)
Red Red Wine (UB40)
Tequila Sunrise (The Eagles)
Beer Drinkers and Hell Raisers (Motorhead)
Spanish Wine (Chris White)
Bordeaux Rosé (Fairfield Parlour)
Escape – The Pina Colada Song (Rupert Holmes)

Ten more ways to leave your lover

Send her a fax, Max
Speak after the tone, Joan
Just change the lock, Jock
Place a small ad, Brad
Use your air miles, Giles
Drop out of sight, Dwight
Phone from Japan, Ann
Tell him the truth, Ruth
Get on your bike, Mike
Get your girl to call his girl, Shirl

Give her a call, Paul

Tammy spells it out

Ten initial hits

Y.M.C.A. (Village People, 1978)
R.S.V.P. (Five Star, 1985)
D.J. (David Bowie, 1979)
F.B.I. (The Shadows, 1961)
I.O.I.O. (Bee Gees, 1970)
T.V. (Flying Lizards, 1980)
D.I.V.O.R.C.E. (Tammy Wynette, 1975)
S.O.S. (Abba, 1975)
I.O.U. (Freez, 1983)
W.O.L.D. (Harry Chapin, 1974)

Deejay-speak – a guide to interpretation

'Here's one we've had tons of requests for': *Two letters and a fax*

'Yeh, Elton's one of the really genuine guys in rock': *Unlike me*

'This is what we in the business call a turntable hit': *Desperate attempt to make playing records sound like a profession*

'Have we got a whole bunch of great sounds for you!': *Have we? I wouldn't know, since my producer chooses the records*

'This BBC coffee could strip asphalt': *Cracks like that didn't do Terry Wogan any harm*

'Let's get on down and groove': *I'm over forty and paranoid about being pensioned off*

'It's going to be twenty-five big ones out there today': *It's going to be 25°C*

'Boy, is it madness in here today, or what!': *I'm doing the show in shorts*

'Let's not forget life's more serious side': *Traffic and weather reports*

'Hey, Julie, Basildon sounds like a great place!': *My middle name is 'patronising'*

Dracula's top ten

Demons are a Girl's Best Friend
I Enjoy being a Ghoul
There is Nothing Like a Damien
Lucifer in the Sky with Demons
Satan Doll
Transylvania 6–5000
My Funny Frankenstein
If My Fiends could See Me Now
Fangs for the Memory
Harpy Days are Here Again

Ten songs they should play when you're hanging on the phone

Could It Be Forever (David Cassidy)
As Time Goes By (Dooley Wilson)
Tired of Waiting for You (Kinks)
You Keep Me Hangin' On (Supremes)
Don't Give Up (Peter Gabriel and Kate Bush)
Can't Wait Another Minute (Five Star)
Money for Nothing (Dire Straits)
Hold the Line (Toto)
Answer Me (Barbara Dickson)
How Long (Rod Stewart)

Engaged – call later

Ten updated Beatles songs

Bus Pass to Ride
Sergeant Pepper's Computer Dating Agency Band
Help Line!
The Ballad of Yoko
Yellow De-Commissioned Submarine
When I'm 84
Let it Lie
Back in the Russian Federation
Nowhere Person
The Long and Grinding Road (M25)

Marital harmony –
ten husband-and-wife hitmakers

Sonny and Cher: *I Got You Babe* (1965)
Ike and Tina Turner: *River Deep Mountain High*
    (1966)
Carly Simon and James Taylor: *Mockingbird*
    (1974)
Esther and Abi Ofarim: *Cinderella Rockefella*
    (1968)
Steve Lawrence and Eydie Gorme: *I Want to Stay
    Here* (1963)
Womack and Womack: *Teardrops* (1988)
Ashford and Simpson: *Solid* (1985)
Captain and Tennille: *Do That to Me One More
    Time* (1980)
Paul and Linda McCartney: *Back Seat of My Car*
    (1971)
Rita Coolidge and Kris Kristofferson: *A Song I'd
    Like to Sing* (1973)

Tracy's kind of guy

Don't give up the day job – ten people
who have appeared in pop videos

Neil Kinnock (*My Guy* by Tracey Ullman)
Ian McKellen (*Heart* by the Pet Shop Boys)
Chevy Chase (*You Can Call Me Al* by Paul Simon)
French & Saunders (*That Ole Devil Called Love* by
    Alison Moyet)
Frances Tomelty (*Sister of Mercy* by The
    Thompson Twins)
Donald Sutherland (*Cloudbusting* by Kate Bush)
Magnus Pyke (*She Blinded Me with Science* by
    Thomas Dolby)
Joss Ackland (*Always on my Mind* by the Pet Shop
    Boys)
Danny De Vito (*When the Going Gets Tough* by
    Billy Ocean)
Frankie Howerd (*Don't Let Me Down* by The
    Farm)

Opera for the masses –
ten plots in a nutshell

Roll-your-own fags girl in stadium stabbing
    (*Carmen*)
Surprise winner of Eurovision song contest (*Die
    Meistersinger*)
Oriental child bride in tug-of-love suicide
    (*Madame Butterfly*)
Trainee shortage threatens east coast fishing
    industry (*Peter Grimes*)
Former call girl dies in love nest (*La Traviata*)
Police slayer in prison roof death plunge (*Tosca*)
Cadet officer in country house bedroom sex-
    change frolic (*The Marriage of Figaro*)
Good neighbour policy fails to save Paris TB
    victim (*La Bohème*)
Three die in mixed marriage handkerchief muddle
    (*Otello*)
Incest offspring to marry aunt (*Siegfried*)

I got you babe

Mary: so near, yet so fair

Eight days a week in song

Lazy Sunday (The Small Faces)
Blue Monday (New Order)
Ruby Tuesday (The Rolling Stones)
Wednesday Week (The Undertones)
Thursday Afternoon (Brian Eno)
Friday on my Mind (The Easybeats)
Another Saturday Night (Sam Cooke)
Sunday Girl (Blondie)

So near, yet so far –
ten UK acts who came second in the Eurovision Song Contest

Pearl Carr and Teddy Johnson: *Sing Little Birdie* (1959)
Matt Monro: *I Love the Little Things* (1964)
Kathy Kirby: *I Belong* (1965)
Cliff Richard: *Congratulations* (1968)
Mary Hopkin: *Knock Knock Who's There?* (1970)
The New Seekers: *Beg Steal or Borrow* (1972)
The Shadows: *Let Me be the One* (1975)
Lynsey De Paul and Mike Moran: *Rock Bottom* (1977)
Scott Fitzgerald: *Go* (1988)
Live Report: *Why Do I Always Get it Wrong?* (1989)

A guide to the Eurovision Song Contest

'Zero points': *Norway*
'International appeal': *Repeats la, la, la*
'National jubilation': *Norway thought it had scored a point*
'Winning formula': *Sound like Buck's Fizz*
'Innovative': *Complete absence of la, la, la*
'Sorry, we can't hear you, Norway': *Sulking*
'Catchy': *La, la, la in Turkish*
'Touching': *Norway tries to vote for itself*
'Patriotic': *German pop group in lederhosen*
'The new Song for Europe': *You have been warned*

Ten countries which have scored zero points in the Eurovision Song Contest

Iceland (*Pam Sem Einginn Ser* by Daniel, 1989)
Austria (*Lisa Mona Lisa* by Wilfried, 1988)
Turkey (*Opera* by Cetin Alp & Shortwave, 1983)
Finland (*Nuku Pommiin* by Kojo, 1982)
Norway (*Aldri I Livet* by Finn Kalvik, 1981)
Luxembourg (*Je Suis Tombé du Ciel* by David Alexander Winter, 1970)
Italy (*Dio Come Te Amo* by Domenico Modugno, 1966)
Monaco (*Bien Plus Fort* by Teresa, 1966)
Spain (*Qué Buento Qué Buento* by Concita Bautista, 1965)
Belgium (*Ton Nom* by Fud Leclerc, 1962)

Madonna: looking for her Man Friday

Ten records which castaways on *Desert Island Discs* should choose

Rescue Me (Madonna)
Help! (The Beatles)
Message in a Bottle (The Police)
All by Myself (Eric Carmen)
Living on an Island (Status Quo)
Save Me (Dave Dee, Dozy, Beaky, Mick and Tich)
I Talk to the Trees (Clint Eastwood)
On the Beach (Cliff Richard)
Alone Again (Naturally) (Gilbert O'Sullivan)
Life on your Own (Human League)

The last ten Christmas number one hit records

Saviour's Day: Cliff Richard (1990)
Do They Know It's Christmas?: Band Aid II (1989)
Mistletoe and Wine: Cliff Richard (1988)
Always on my Mind: Pet Shop Boys (1987)
Caravan of Love: The Housemartins (1986)
Saving all my Love for You: Whitney Houston (1985)
Do They Know It's Christmas?: Band Aid (1984)
Only You: Flying Pickets (1983)
Save Your Love: Renée and Renato (1982)
Don't You Want Me: Human League (1981)

A travelling salesman's top ten

Kendal in the Wind
Nothing Compares to Crewe
Ticket to Ryde
Lady in Reading
Three Steps to Devon
A Whiter Shade of Poole
All You Need is Hove
What have I done to Deserve Diss?
Keep Brighton to the End of the Road
Something in the Ayr

Sing something simple-minded – ten memorable song titles

I'd rather be a Lobster than a Wiseguy (Edward Madden and Theodore F Morse, 1907)
Who ate Napoleons with Josephine when Bonaparte was Away (Alfred Bryan and E Ray Gotz, 1920)
Hey Young Fella Close your Old Umbrella (Dorothy Fields and Jimmy McHugh, 1933)
All the Quakers are Shoulder Shakers down in Quaker Town (Bert Kalmar, Edgar Leslie and Pete Wendling, 1919)
You're just a little Nigger, still you're mine, all mine (Paul Dresser, 1898)
Potatoes are Cheaper, Tomatoes are Cheaper, Now's the Time to Fall in Love (Al Lewis and Al Sherman, 1931)
Caledonia, what makes your Big Head so Hard (Fleecie Moore, 1946)
I Love to Dunk a Hunk of Sponge Cake (Clarence Gaskill, 1928)
Hang your Heart on a Hickory Limb (Johnny Burke and James V Monaco, 1939)
Aunt Jemima and your Uncle Cream of Wheat (Johnny Mercer and Rube Bloom, 1936)

Ten songs for weathermen

It might as well Rain until September (Carole King)
Hot in the City (Billy Idol)
Here Comes the Rain Again (Eurythmics)
Lightnin' Strikes (Lou Christie)
Grey Day (Madness)
Ain't no Sunshine (Michael Jackson)
Sunshine on Leith (Proclaimers)
It's Raining Again (Supertramp)
One Fine Day (Chiffons)
Wild is the Wind (David Bowie)

Never mind the music – get a load of the album title

My People were Fair and Had Sky in their Hair But Now they're Content to Wear Stars on their Brows (Tyrannosaurus Rex)
Lick my Decals off Baby (Captain Beefheart and his Magic Band)
Dirk Wears White Sox (Adam and the Ants)
5,000 Spirits or the Layers of the Onion (The Incredible String Band)
Quark Strangeness and Charm (Hawkwind)
See Jungle! See Jungle! Go Join your Gang Yeah City All Over! Go Ape Crazy! (Bow Wow Wow)
Smell the Glove (Spinal Tap)
Larks' Tongues in Aspic (King Crimson)
The North Star Grassman and the Ravens (Sandy Denny)
Hot Rats (Frank Zappa)

They're playing their song – DJs who have made records

Mike Read (*High Rise*)
Steve Wright (*I'm Alright*)
Paul Burnett and Dave Lee Travis (*Convoy GB*)
Tony Blackburn (*So Much Love*)
Liz Kershaw and Bruno Brookes (*It Takes Two*)
Noel Edmunds (*I Wanna be a Winner*)
Terry Wogan (*The Floral Dance*)
Jimmy Young (*Unchained Melody*)
Mick Brown and Pat Sharp (*Let's All Chant*)
Kenny Everett (*Snot Rap*)

Jason and Kylie clean up

The Kylie and Jason factor – ten soap stars who have made records

Malandra Burrows (Kathy Merrick in *Emmerdale*): *Just this Side of Love*
Anita Dobson (Angie Watts in *EastEnders*): *Anyone Can Fall in Love*
Danny McCall (Owen in *Brookside*): *Whose Heart is it Anyway*
Nick Berry (Wicksy in *EastEnders*): *Every Loser Wins*
Stefan Dennis (Paul Robinson in *Neighbours*): *Don't it Make You Feel Good*
Sue Nicholls (Audrey Roberts in *Coronation Street*): *Where Will You Be*
Danii Minogue (Emma in *Home and Away*): *Love and Kisses*
Wendy Richard (Pauline Fowler in *EastEnders*): *Come Outside*
Trevor Harrison (Eddie Grundy in *The Archers*): *Lambs to the Slaughter*
Tom Watt (Lofty in *EastEnders*): *Subterranean Homesick Blues*

Not wanted, even with a bad ear

Sick songs – ten record requests hospital radio should ignore

The First Cut is the Deepest (Rod Stewart)
Take My Heart (Kool and the Gang)
Another One Bites The Dust (Queen)
Be Stiff (Devo)
Help Me Make It through the Night (Gladys Knight and the Pips)
Do You Really Want to Hurt Me (Culture Club)
Take My Breath Away (Berlin)
Cold as Ice (Foreigner)
When I'm Dead and Gone (McGuinness Flint)
Bye Bye Love (Everly Brothers)

Ten numbers that made the charts

5.15 (The Who)
5-4-3-2-1 (Manfred Mann)
20/20 (George Benson)
634-5789 (Wilson Pickett)
007 (Musical Youth)
5-7-0-5 (City Boy)
98.6 (Keith)
1-2-3 (Len Barry)
99½ (Carol Lynn Townes)
1999 (Prince and The Revolution)

Ten songs for Levi's commercials

Baggy Trousers (Madness)
Fattie Bum Bum (Carl Malcolm)
Blue Turns to Grey (Cliff Richard)
Bell Bottom Blues (Derek and the Dominos)
Every Which Way but Loose (Eddie Rabbit)
Fat Bottomed Girls (Queen)
Something's Gotta Give (Sammy Davis Jr)
Can't Keep It In (Cat Stevens)
Matchstalk Men and Matchstalk Cats and Dogs (Brian and Michael)
Tangled Up in Blue (Bob Dylan)

A footballers' top ten

Soccer round the Clock (Bill Haley and the Comets)
Indifferent Corner (George Michael)
Let's get Physio (Olivia Newton-John)
Willie and the Handball (Cliff Richard)
Foul on the Hill (The Beatles)
It's Training Again (Supertramp)
Waiting for a Goal like You (Foreigner)
Midfield Sprain for Georgie (Gladys Knight and the Pips)
Jeepers Creepers Where d'you Get those Sweepers (Mel Torme)
Header over Heels (Tears For Fears)

George Michael: no Faith as a footballer?

Vive les pop charts –
ten French songs which were UK hits

Ca Plane Pour Moi (Plastic Bertrand, 1978)
Je T'Aime . . . Moi Non Plus (Jane Birkin and
    Serge Gainsbourg, 1969)
Dominique (Singing Nun, 1963)
La Dernière Valse (Mireille Mathieu, 1967)
Tous les Garçons et les Filles (Françoise Hardy,
    1964)
Et les Oiseaux Chantaient (Sweet People, 1980)
L'Oiseau et l'Enfant (Marie Myriam, 1977)
Un Banc, Un Arbre, Une Rue (Severine, 1971)
Joe le Taxi (Vanessa Paradis, 1988)
Milord (Edith Piaf, 1960)

Rock revival –
ten bands for a 90s nostalgia tour

Adam and the Antiques
UB65
Grey Floyd
The Grandmothers of Invention
Stiffer Little Fingers
The Trembeloes
Thirty Years After
The Grandmamas and Grandpapas
Dr Feelbad
Gerry and the Pacemakers

The loon's a balloon

Dross of the pops –
ten naff lines from pop songs

'He starts to shake, he starts to cough / Just like the
    old man in that famous book by Nabokov'
    (*Don't Stand So Close to Me*, The Police)
'What's it like to be a loon? / I liken it to a balloon'
    (*Cosmic Dancer*, Marc Bolan)
'I am I said to no one there / And no one heard at
    all not even the chair' (*I Am . . . I Said*, Neil
    Diamond)
'Between the parted pages and were pressed in
    love's hot fevered iron like a striped pair of
    pants' (*Macarthur Park*, Richard Harris)
'Don't want to be in public / My head is full of
    chopstick / I don't like it' (*Cracks in the
    Pavement*, Duran Duran)
'In the desert you can remember your name /
    Cause there ain't no one for to give you no pain'
    (*A Horse With No Name*, America)
'I sat on the roof / And kicked off the moss / Well a
    few of the verses / Well they've got me quite
    cross' (*Your Song*, Elton John)
'One of sixteen vestal virgins who were leaving for
    the coast / And although my eyes were open
    they might just have well been closed' (*A Whiter
    Shade of Pale*, Procol Harum)
'I pine a lot / I find the lot / Falls through without
    you' (*Wuthering Heights*, Kate Bush)
'Husbands moan at breakfast tables / No milk, no
    eggs, no marmalade labels' (*Excerpt From a
    Teenage Opera*, Keith West)

THE MEDIA

The ten most common items on *That's Life*

Rude vegetables
Crossbred terriers with an O-level in maths
Telephone bills to people who died twenty years
   ago
Large ladies impersonating foghorns
People who can pull their lower lip over their head
Income tax reminders to eight-month-old children
Parrots who can play *When the Saints come*
   Marching in on the trombone
People whose fillings can pick up Radio Moscow
Couples who have been conned out of their life
   savings
Children with musical ear lobes

The first ten commercials to appear on ITV

Gibbs SR toothpaste
Cadbury's drinking chocolate
Kraft cheeses
Dunlop tyres
Woman magazine
Surf washing powder
National Benzole petrol
Lux soap
Ford cars
Guinness

'It's your line to . . .'
A guide to radio phone-ins

'Remember, this is your show': *Dead cheap to produce*

'I'll just turn to our studio guest for a moment': *No calls*

'Our lines are open and we're waiting to hear from you': *I won't tell you again*

'I'm sure you've all got views on this controversial subject': *Is anybody out there?*

'I think you've made your point': *Get off the line*

'It's obviously a subject close to your heart': *Totally beyond reason*

'You seem to know a lot about this issue': *Makes a refreshing change*

'Would you care to elaborate on your views?': *Ten minutes to go and no other callers in prospect*

'It's good to get the woman's point of view': *Wife of the man who was cut off earlier*

'You're one of our regular callers, aren't you?': *It's that old bigot again*

Do they mean me?

Let's parlez Jameson –
a beginners' guide

'Moaning': *Good morning*

'Goad': *Precious metal, as in 'worth its weight in goad'*

'Me you': *Advisable to eat three square ones a day*

'Owed': *Getting on in years*

'Wold': *Particularly useful for introducing the New Seekers' chart-topping hit,* I'd Like to Teach the Wold to Sing

'Nooz': *The serious bit at the top of the hour about wold events*

'Code': *They still haven't found a cure for the common one*

'Go': *What Gary Lineker occasionally scores*

'Paw': *As in 'Paw McCartney'*

'Toad': *As in 'I toad you so'*

Ten scoops *Hello!* missed

Adolf and Eva welcome us into their magnificent bunker and speak about their plans for the future

Grigori Rasputin shows us round his tastefully appointed rooms and talks openly about his 'bad boy' image

The Marquis de Sade invites us into his sumptuous games room and reveals some interesting tips for marital happiness

Jack the Ripper takes us on a tour of undiscovered Whitechapel and hits back at his critics

Count Dracula opens his satin-lined coffin and tells us why he's at his best as a 'night person'

Dr Hawley Crippen greets us in his minimalist cell and speaks touchingly about life without his wife

Josef Stalin launches his Gulag Holiday Camps and takes time out to tell us of his hopes for tractor production in Georgia

Genghis Khan relaxes in his exquisite designer tent and explains why he's been misunderstood

King Herod speaks frankly about the strains of royal duties and tells us of his sadness at the children he lost

Josef Goebbels shows us round 'his' Nuremberg and gives us his special recipe for cabbage rolls

Brookspeak: a *gaeed* to interpretation

A handy glossary for *Brookside* viewers

'Bare': *Liquid refreshment bought in cans at the off-licence*

'Where'k': *Something people do when not on the dole*

'Turkey': *Popular holiday resort on the Devon coast, near Turbay*

'Bias': *Common greeting on entering a pub, as in 'Bias a pint'*

'Meeman': *Woman in an apron, often to be found weeping in the kitchen about 'meekids'*

'Wezmeedinna?': *Have you made me anything to eat?*

'Amoff': *I'm leaving, as in 'After meedinna amoff down the pub'*

'Nuttin': *Not a thing, as in 'There's nuttin on the telly'*

'Scurred': *Somewhat worried*

'Summit': *Tangible entity, as in 'There's summit jammed in me ear'*

TV mini-series cast call

English rose (Jane Seymour)
Cameo appearance (Sir John Gielgud)
Handsome priest struggling with his vows (Richard Chamberlain)
Emotionally repressed Englishman (Christopher Cazenove)
Mid-Atlantic heroine (Stefanie Powers)
Woman of a certain age (Kate O'Mara)
Immaculately preserved head of international business empire (Deborah Kerr)
The other woman (Stephanie Beacham)
Fading matinée idol (Stewart Granger)
Man in cravat and tennis sweater (Nigel Havers)

Oo-er, missus – ten joke topics which used to be banned by the BBC

Lavatories
Effeminacy in men
Honeymoon couples
Fig leaves
Commercial travellers
Ladies' underwear
Lodgers
Chambermaids
Animal habits
The word 'basket'

Newspaper obituaries –
a guide to interpretation

'Lived life to the full': *Married five times*

'Enjoyed a varied career': *Couldn't keep a job*

'Didn't suffer fools gladly': *Arrogant sod*

'Suffered a number of setbacks': *Done for fraud*

'Never fulfilled his early promise': *Fell prey to the demon drink*

'One of a kind': *Thank God*

'Displayed one or two eccentricities in later years': *Completely bonkers*

'His early work will guarantee him a place in history': *Had one good idea*

'Never married': *Say no more*

'Distinguished career': *Was never found out*

Magazines for the modern man –
a guide to contents

'Getting your life in order': *Cataloguing your bow ties*

'Going back to basics': *Living in a converted warehouse*

'Essential accessory': *£180 leather pouch for your breath fresheners*

'Making a statement': *Wearing yellow socks*

'Wet dreams': *Speedboat racing*

'Modern master': *Giorgio Armani*

'Spirit of the age': *Aqua Libra*

'Living dangerously': *Tweed jacket with houndstooth-check waistcoat*

'Sex object': *Sports car*

'Women we love': *We're not all gay, you know*

Are you cut out to be a TV weatherman? Ten tell-tale signs

You have the dress sense of a door-to-door brush salesman

You spend hours in front of the mirror practising the phrase: 'And that's it from me'

You wouldn't mind being the one on the extreme left in TV panel game shows

You have a definite flair for the mundane

You are prepared to take personal responsibility for bad weather

You have a clear understanding of the difference between sunny periods with occasional showers, and showery periods with occasional sunshine

You can remember the formula for converting Fahrenheit into centigrade

You can sweep your arm over a map of Europe with great authority

You can stand the pressure of bringing us the bad news at the start of every bank holiday

You find satellite pictures more meaningful than just a lot of off-white swirly bits

More interesting than the weatherman

Cliff: the man from never never land

Media shorthand –
a guide to interpretation
'The Peter Pan of pop': *Cliff Richard*
'The nation's favourite granny': *The Queen Mother*
'Wacky DJ': *Kenny Everett*
'Zany comedienne': *Ruby Wax*
'Controversial judge': *James Pickles*
'Retired judge': *Lord Denning*
'Soccer's wayward genius': *George Best*
'Controversial clergyman': *The Bishop of Durham*
'Wacko popstar': *Michael Jackson*
'The new Olivier': *Kenneth Branagh*

Game show-speak –
a guide to interpretation
'Dream prize': *Teak veneered hostess trolley*
'The audience is right behind you': *Gasps when contestant guesses the capital of Belgium*
'Very nearly': *Maurice Chevalier is not the President of France*
'Just try to relax': *Only ten million viewers are watching*
'Can you come back next week?': *Can you wait for ten minutes while I change my jacket and we record another show?*
'Good answer': *You correctly remembered your name*
'Celebrity panel': *Has-been stars desperate for publicity*
'This could be your lucky night': *To be humiliated*
'Take your time over this one': *Who is the Prime Minister of Britain?*
'You're not feeling nervous, are you?': *Desperate attempt to build up tension*

Déjà view – a guide to interpretation
'Old favourite': *Repeat*
'First shown on BBC2': *Repeat*
'Another chance to see': *Repeat*
'Retrospective season': *Lots of repeats*
'Tribute': *Repeated repeat*
'Highlights': *Bits of repeats cobbled together*
'*Late Again*': *Unashamed repeated highlights*
'Satellite TV': *24 hours of repeats*
'*The Great Escape*': *The ultimate repeat*
'Classic': *Repeat repeated so often the colour has faded*

. . . and over in the garden

Are you sitting comfortably? Ten quotes about television

'Imitation is the sincerest form of television' (Fred Allen)

'Television is an invention that permits you to be entertained in your living-room by people you wouldn't have in your home' (David Frost)

'I like to talk on TV about those things which aren't worth writing about' (Truman Capote)

'Television – the longest amateur night in history' (Robert Carson)

'Television is a medium, so called because it is neither rare nor well done!' (Ernie Kovacs)

'Television has proved that people will look at anything rather than each other' (Ann Landers)

'Television is chewing-gum for the eyes' (Frank Lloyd Wright)

'Television is more interesting than people – if it were not, we should have people standing in the corners of our rooms' (Alan Coren)

'Television – the bland leading the bland' (Anon)

'I hate television, I hate it as much as peanuts. But I can't stop eating peanuts' (Orson Welles)

Create your own daytime TV programme – ten ideas you'll need

Celebrity gardening spot with Penelope Keith
Latest single performed by The Nolans
Exclusive in-depth interview with Judy Carne
The Duchess of Kent attending a Gilbert and Sullivan operetta at a youth centre
Celebrity cookery spot with Derek Nimmo
A comic interlude with Stan Boardman
Leslie Thomas talking about his latest book
Susan Hampshire telling us about a new project to help dyslexics
Coffee on the sofa with Beryl Reid
Nanette Newman shows us her collection of children's poems

The ten longest-running programmes on radio

Choral Evensong (1926)
Daily Service (1928)
The Week in Westminster (1929)
Desert Island Discs (1942)
Saturday Night Theatre (1943)
This Week's Composer (1943)
From Our Own Correspondent (1946)
Woman's Hour (1946)
Down Your Way (1946)
Letter From America (1946)

David Frost, allowed in through the keyhole

Vital statistics – in an average life, you will . . .

Spend 12 years watching television
Use 2,574 rolls of toilet paper
Walk 150,000 miles
Eat 7,800 loaves of bread
Sleep for 25 years
Take 13,650 baths
Shed 300lb of skin
Go through 675 pairs of underpants
Blink 682 million times
Flush the lavatory 109,200 times

Licking the back of Marilyn Monroe – ten celebrities who have appeared on postage stamps

John Lennon (Maldive Islands)
James Cagney (Dominica)
Ian Botham (St Vincent)
Charlie Chaplin (Gambia)
David Niven (Lesotho)
Margaret Thatcher (Kenya)
Muhammad Ali (Liberia)
Rudolph Nureyev (San Marino)
Evlis Presley (St Vincent)
Marilyn Monroe (Antigua and Barbuda)

The Post Office's top-selling special stamp issues

European nature conservation (May 1986)
British butterflies (May 1981)
150th anniversary of the RSPCA's Royal Charter (January 1990)
Flowers (March 1979)
Centenary of the Shire Horse Society of England (July 1978)
Centenary of the Wild Bird Protection Act (January 1980)
Dogs (February 1979)
Centenary of the RSPB (January 1989)
Queen Mother's 80th birthday (August 1980)
The wedding of Prince Charles and Lady Diana (July 1981)

Ten people who appeared as themselves in soap operas

Harold Macmillan (*The Archers*)
Paula Yates (*Brookside*)
Freddie Trueman (*Emmerdale*)
Princess Margaret (*The Archers*)
Bernard Manning (*Coronation Street*)
The Duke of Westminster (*The Archers*)
Russell Grant (*Brookside*)
Arthur Marshall (*Crossroads*)
The Duke of Bedford (*Coronation Street*)
Humphrey Lyttleton (*The Archers*)

Billy: and there's space in the back for the kids

Ten couples whose children attended their wedding

Chris Eubank and Karron Stephen-Martin (Christopher)
Paul Young and Stacey Smith (Levi)
Mick Jagger and Jerry Hall (Scarlett and James)
Richard Branson and Joan Templeman (Holly and Sam)
Billy Connolly and Pamela Stephenson (Amy, Daisy and Scarlett)
Diego Maradona and Claudia Villafane (Dalma and Giannina)
Bob Geldof and Paula Yates (Fifi)
Neneh Cherry and Cameron McVey (Naima and Tyson)
Frank Bruno and Laura Mooney (Nicola and Rachel)
John Barnes and Suzy Bicknell (Jamie and Jordan)

Ten people who have insured parts of their body

Keith Richard: the third finger of his left hand for £1m
Bruce Springsteen: his voice for £3.5m
Jamie Lee Curtis: her legs for £1.5m
Dolly Parton: her chest for £2m
Nigel Benn: his fists for £10m
Morgan Fairchild: her hands and feet for £2m
Merv Hughes: his moustache for £200,000
Ken Dodd: his teeth for £4m
Mark King: his hands for £1m
Suzanne Mizzi: her chest for £2m

Paula: no problem with bridesmaids

Purdey and Steed – write on

Lest we forget – ten TV series which still have fan clubs

The Saint
The Prisoner
Crossroads
The Avengers
Randall and Hopkirk (Deceased)
V
Poldark
The A-Team
Scarecrow and Mrs King
Auf Wiedersehen Pet

Budget bits and bobs

The word 'budget' comes from the French 'bougette', meaning a little bag

The first Budget speech was given by Sir Robert Walpole in 1733

The longest Budget speech, four hours forty-five minutes, was delivered by Gladstone in 1853

Only one Budget debate has been suspended, when Nigel Lawson was shouted down in 1988

Sir Alexander Mackintosh, a journalist, holds the record for listening to the most Budget speeches – sixty from 1881 to 1941

One Chancellor forgot to take his Budget speech to the Commons – Ward Hunt in 1868

James Callaghan is the only Chancellor not to carry his speech in the famous red box

The shortest Budget speech, forty-five minutes, was delivered by Disraeli in 1867

The only Budget to be overturned this century was Lloyd George's in 1909

Only one Chancellor, James Callaghan, worked for the Inland Revenue

Ten of this year's lesser known anniversaries

200 years ago the first successful dentures were patented by Nicholas de Chemant

150 years ago the first detective story, *The Murders in the Rue Morgue* by Edgar Allen Poe, was published

150 years ago Britain's first ice-skating rink, the Glaciarium, opened in Regent's Park

150 years ago the chest expander was patented by William Baillieur

100 years ago the first penalty kick in an English Football League match was awarded to Wolverhampton Wanderers against Accrington

100 years ago American Express travellers' cheques were used for the first time

100 years ago the first tins of baked beans in tomato sauce were manufactured

75 years ago Annette Kellerman became the first film star to appear naked on screen in *Daughter of the Gods*

75 years ago false eyelashes were worn for the first time

25 years ago the ring-pull can made its first appearance

Look, who's doing the talking?

Making monkeys of themselves – ten people who did voice overs for the PG Tips chimps

Peter Sellers
Stanley Baxter
Arthur Lowe
Bruce Forsyth
Pat Coombs
Kenneth Connor
Irene Handl
Bob Monkhouse
Kenneth Williams
Michael Jayston

Bar charts – Britain's ten oldest chocolate bars

Fry's Chocolate Cream (1875)
Cadbury's Dairy Milk (1905)
Cadbury's Bournville (1908)
Cadbury's Flake (1911)
Fry's Turkish Delight (1914)
Cadbury's Fruit & Nut (1921)
Terry's 1767 Bitter Bar (1922)
Cadbury's Crunchie (1929)
Cadbury's Whole Nut (1930)
Terry's Waifa Bar (1934)

Death, here is thy sting – ten ignoble ways to go

Charles VIII of France died after hitting his head on a low doorway in 1498
Frederick, Prince of Wales, died after being hit on the head by a cricket ball in 1751
King John died after eating vast quantities of peaches and cider in 1216
Lady Coventry died after using white lead as a cosmetic to paint her face in 1760
The Duke of Clarence drowned in a cask of sweet wine in 1478
George I of England died of apoplexy after eating too many melons in 1727
King Haakon VII of Norway died after falling into his bath in 1957
King Alexander of Greece died after being bitten by his pet monkey in 1920
Henry I of England died after eating too many lampreys (eel-like fish) in 1135
Edward II of England was disembowelled with a red-hot poker in 1327

Sir Clement, endorsing a sandwich

Order, order (while stocks last) – ten politicians who have appeared in advertisements

Sir David Steel (National Westminster Bank)
Sir Cyril Smith (Access)
Ken Livingstone (National Dairy Council Cheeses)
Ronald Reagan (General Electric)
Lord George-Brown (Normandy Ferries)
Sir Merlyn Rees (Bananarama Greatest Hits)
Sir Clement Freud (Chunky Dog Food and Minced Morsels)
Lord Gormley (Cadbury's Chocolate Buttons)
Ron Brown (Bananarama's Greatest Hits)
Edward Heath (National Dairy Council Cheeses)

Life before Morse – ten actors who appeared in *The Avengers*

John Thaw
Peter Bowles
Penelope Keith
John Cleese
Kate O'Mara
Donald Sutherland
Warren Mitchell
Charlotte Rampling
Ronnie Barker
Frank Windsor

Ten time-serving statesmen

Konrad Adenauer, Chancellor of West Germany (retired aged 87)
Eamon De Valera, President of Eire (retired aged 90)
Marshal Tito, President of Yugoslavia (died in office aged 87)
Urho Kekkonen, President of Finland (resigned aged 81)
Morarji Desai, Prime Minister of India (electoral defeat aged 84)
General Franco of Spain (died in office aged 82)
Jomo Kenyatta, President of Kenya (died in office aged 80)
Winston Churchill, Prime Minister of Great Britain (retired aged 80)
Deng Xiaoping, Party General Secretary of China (retired aged 83)
Field Marshal Hindenburg, President of Germany (died in office aged 87)

Ten insignificant numbers

336 (*dimples on a golf ball*)
50 (*eggs eaten in an hour by Paul Newman in* Cool Hand Luke)
206 (*bones in an adult human body*)
4,280 (*buffaloes killed by William 'Buffalo Bill' Cody*)
227 (*different ways to cook chicken, according to Escoffer's* Le Guide Culinaire, *1921*)
775,692 (*words in the King James version of* The Bible)
600 (*ways of making love, according to the Marquis de Sade*)
24 (*dollar value of the trinkets paid to the Indians in 1626 for Manhattan Island*)
277 (*mountains in Scotland over 3,000 feet*)
20,000 (*pieces Lenin's brain was cut into for research purposes after his death*)

A car by any other name – ten alternative names which were considered for the Metro

Mini Tiger
Minion
Novamini
Mini Mate
Midi
Ergo Mini
Epic
Mini Magnet
Economini
Mini Jag

Mini Magnet by another name

G133 BRW

Now here's a funny thing – former occupations of ten comedians

Lennie Bennett (journalist)
Marti Caine (model)
Jackie Mason (rabbi)
Russ Abbot (drummer)
Dawn French (teacher)
Bernard Manning (cigarette factory worker)
Gareth Hale (PE teacher)
Alexei Sayle (art college lecturer)
Benny Hill (milkman)
Helen Lederer (social worker)

Bennie as Ernie: life imitating art?

Where there's life there's soap – ten actors who have made a career out of it

Wendy Richard: Joyce Harker in *The Newcomers*, Pauline Fowler in *EastEnders*
Alan Rothwell: David Barlow in *Coronation Street*, Nicholas Black in *Brookside*
Graham Seed: Nigel Pargetter in *The Archers*, Charlie Mycroft in *Crossroads*
Malandra Burrows: Lisa in *Brookside*, Kathy Bates in *Emmerdale*
Ronald Allen: Ian Harman in *Compact*, David Hunter in *Crossroads*
Betty Alberge: Florrie Lindley in *Coronation Street*, Edna Cross in *Brookside*
Gabrielle Drake: Inga Olsen in *Coronation Street*, Nicola Freeman in *Crossroads*
Tony Adams: Dr Bywaters in *General Hospital*, Adam Chance in *Crossroads*
Diana Davis: Norma Ford in *Coronation Street*, Mrs Bates in *Emmerdale*
Jane Rossington: Monica Downes in *The Archers*, Jill Chance in *Crossroads*

A youth making up for lost time

Ten curious pub names

Jolly Taxpayer (Portsmouth)
Nobody Inn (London)
Blazing Donkey (Ramsgate)
Ladas (Epsom)
Queen's Head and Artichoke (London)
Help Me Through This World (Bury)
Chalk Drawers (Colney Heath)
Waste Dealers Arms (Oldham)
Gigolos (Boston)
Shrew Beshrewed (Hersden)

'We are quite amused!' Ten inventions that might have tickled Queen Victoria

Carpet sweeper (Melvin R Bissell, 1876)
Cash register (James Ritty, 1879)
Burglar alarm (Edwin T Holmes, 1858)
Electric iron (H W Seely, 1882)
Fountain pen (Lewis Waterman, 1884)
Elevator (Elisha Otis, 1857)
Linoleum (Frederick Walton, 1860)
Safety pin (Walter Hunt, 1849)
Bicycle (Kirkpatrick Macmillan, 1840)
Safety razor (King C Gillette, 1895)

The ten ages of youth

Aged 4: can travel in the front seat of a car wearing an adult seat belt
Aged 5: can drink alcohol legally
Aged 10: can be held responsible for a criminal act
Aged 12: can buy a pet without a parent being present
Aged 13: can take a part-time job
Aged 14: can play dominoes or cribbage in a pub
Aged 16: can sell scrap metal
Aged 17: can apply for a helicopter pilot's licence
Aged 18: can be tattooed
Aged 21: can adopt a child

'My Dad was . . .'
Ten fathers of the famous

A pawnbroker (Norman Tebbit)
A crane driver (Michael Jackson)
A Labour MP (Fred Perry)
Owner of a Soho wrestling club (David Bowie)
A surgical goods retailer (Benny Hill)
A PE teacher (Mick Jagger)
A bookmaker (Albert Finney)
A meteorologist (Frank Zappa)
A crucifix salesman (Roseanne Barr)
An upholsterer (Frank Bough)

Cuisine poseur – ten celebrities who have written cookbooks

Len Deighton: *The ABC of French Food*
Jane Asher: *Jane Asher's Quick Party Cakes*
Lindsay Wagner: *The High Road to Health: A Vegetarian Cookbook*
Floella Benjamin: *Caribbean Cookery*
George Baker: *A Cook for All Seasons*
Molly Keane: *Molly Keane's Nursery Cookbook*
Linda McCartney: *Home Cooking*
Nanette Newman: *Summer Cookpot*
Tessie O'Shea: *The Slimmer's Cookbook*
The Duchess of Argyll: *My Dinner Party Book*

This is your codename – ten codenames used for targets of the *This Is Your Life* team

Cracker (Frank Carson)
Powder (Stephanie Beacham)
Attack (Rod Hull)
Lawn (Patrick Mower)
Yeast (Jean Boht)
Jacket (Phil Collins)
Beach (Sandy Gall)
Drake (Clare Francis)
Dan (Jeffrey Archer)
Burger (Trevor McDonald)

'Apart from The Bible and Shakespeare': ten books chosen by *Desert Island Discs* castaways

Robinson Crusoe by Daniel Defoe (Leslie Grantham)
Wilt by Tom Sharpe (Steve Davis)
Huckleberry Finn by Mark Twain (Arthur Scargill)
The Times Concise Atlas (Gary Glitter)
Arabian Nights (Salman Rushdie)
Aesop's Fables (Cilla Black)
The Reader's Digest New DIY Manual (Duchess of Kent)
War and Peace by Leo Tolstoy (Princess Margaret)
Mrs Beeton's Household Management (Zandra Rhodes)
The Picture of Dorian Gray by Oscar Wilde (Anita Dobson)

'Apart from The Bible and Shakespeare': ten people who chose Dickens novels on *Desert Island Discs*

Frankie Howerd: *David Copperfield*
Eric Clapton: *Barnaby Rudge*
Ernie Wise: *The Mystery of Edwin Drood*
Robert Robinson: *The Pickwick Papers*
Julian Symons: *Bleak House*
Jack Warner: *A Tale of Two Cities*
Jonathon Porritt: *Bleak House*
Dick Emery: *A Christmas Carol*
Sir Learie Constantine: *The Old Curiosity Shop*
Tom Courtenay: *Great Expectations*

Ten other things which happened on the day President Kennedy was shot (November 22, 1963)

Aldous Huxley died

Benjamin Britten celebrated his fiftieth birthday with a special performance of his opera, *Gloriana*, at the Royal Festival Hall

The Beatles were at No. 1 with *She Loves You*

Denys Lasdun was named as the architect to design the new National Theatre

Britain's oldest MP, David Logan, Labour member for the Scotland division of Liverpool, was ninety-two

Britain claimed sovereignty over an area of the North Sea which contained 'hoped-for oil, gas and coal riches'

The *Daily Mirror* was rapped by the Press Council for a front-page report headed 'Prince Philip and the Profumo Scandal. Rumour is Utterly Unfounded'

Vivien Merchant was named best TV actress of the year by the Guild of TV Producers and Directors for her performance in *The Lover*, written by her husband Harold Pinter

Graeme Pollock scored 120 for South Africa against New South Wales

Vauxhall production workers were offered pay rises of between 5s (25p) and 15s (75p) a week

Light and day . . .

. . . hiss off

Ten people who went mad

Robert Schumann
Friedrich Nietzsche
Zelda Fitzgerald
Beau Brummell
Richard Dadd
August Strindberg
Bedrich Smetana
George III
John Clare
Vaclav Nijinski

Ten phobias suffered by the famous

Ornithophobia (fear of birds): Anne Robinson
Nyctophobia (fear of the dark): Joan Collins
Agoraphobia (fear of open spaces): Aretha Franklin
Phonophobia (fear of loud noises): Julie Andrews
Brontophobia (fear of thunder): Madonna
Ophidiophobia (fear of snakes): Duchess of York
Claustrophobia (fear of enclosed spaces): Simon Ward
Acrophobia (fear of heights): Prince
Aerophobia (fear of flying): Kate Bush
Monophobia (fear of being alone): George Peppard

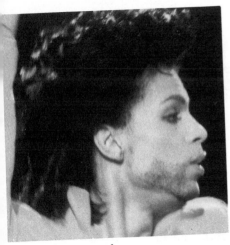

Prince: regal, not naval

Tracy: remembering the good old days

Ten people who lost their surnames

Prince (Nelson)
Dion (DiMucci)
Michelangelo (Buonarroti)
Fabian (Bonaparte)
Madonna (Ciccone)
Donovan (Leitch)
Rembrandt (van Rijn)
Melanie (Safka)
Little Richard (Penniman)
Vangelis (Papathanassiou)

Ten child prodigies

Chopin published his first musical composition, *Polonaise in G Minor*, at the age of seven

Jean Piaget, the child psychologist wrote his first scientific paper at the age of six

Tracy Austin appeared on the cover of *World Tennis* magazine when she was four

Philosopher John Stuart Mill could read English and Greek fluently by the time he was three

Prokofiev wrote an opera, *The Giant*, when he was seven

Judit Polgar won the 1986 New York open chess championship at the age of nine

Daniel Barenboim gave his first public piano recital at the age of seven

Haroldson Lafayette Hunt, once the world's richest man, was reading the financial pages by the age of three

Alfred Lord Tennyson composed a 6,000-word poem when he was ten

Yehudi Menuhin made his stage debut at the age of seven

LITERATURE

So you want to write a whodunnit? Ten characters you must include

A bitter estate owner confined to a wheelchair after a hunting accident

His young wife, who spends all day drinking cocktails by the swimming pool

A mixed-up daughter who takes drugs

A weak and neurotic son who can never live up to his father's expectations

A hatchet-faced housekeeper who wears black and a built-up shoe

A simple-minded stable lad who holds the key to the mystery, but doesn't realise it

A police inspector who is marginally less simple-minded than the stable lad

Someone, possibly a racing driver, who is having an affair with the wife

A brilliantly clever house guest, who solves murders in his or her spare time

A dead body

Guaranteed royalties – ten regal contributions to literature

Budgie the Helicopter (Duchess of York)
A Question of Balance (Prince Philip)
A Vision of Britain (Prince Charles)
The Heart Has Its Reasons (Duchess of Windsor)
A Counterblast on the Use of Tobacco (James I)
Our Life in the Highlands (Queen Victoria)
For My Grandchildren (Princess Alice)
Crowned in a Far Country (Princess Michael of Kent)
The King's Story (Edward VIII)
The Old Man of Lochnagar (Prince Charles)

Prince Charles proving there's nothing like a good book

Ten cherished titles from the poet McGonagall

The Wreck of the Steamer *London* while on her
way to Australia
The Horrors of Majuba
The Tragic Death of the Rev A H Mackonochie
Beautiful Torquay
The Distasterous Fire at Scarborough
Lines in Reply to the Beautiful Poet, who
Welcomed News of McGonagall's Departure
from Dundee
The Great Yellow River Inundation in China
The Wreck of the Barque *Lynton* while Bound for
Aspinwall, Having on Board 1000 Tons of Coal
Lines in Memoriam Regarding the Entertainment
I Gave on the 31st March, 1893, in Reform
Street Hall, Dundee
Nora, the Maid of Killarney

God helps those . . .

Self-help books in a nutshell

Fat is a Feminist Issue: Carry on pigging yourself
What Every Woman Needs to Know about Men:
They all think they're Tom Selleck
*How to Make Love to the Same Man for the Rest of
Your Life*: Imagine he's Tom Selleck
Colour Me Beautiful: Stop wearing jaundice
yellow culottes
Superwoman: How to have a nervous breakdown
in twenty chapters
The Green Consumer Guide: How to be greener-
than-thou
The Joy of Sex: The gourmet's guide
Jane Fonda's Workout Book: Discover God
through the burn
How to Win Friends and Influence People: Be an
insufferable little bastard
How to Survive the Recession: Write a money-
making book like this

Romeo and Juliet: hot off the (olive) press

Shakespeare latest – read all about it

'I deserved all I got' admits battered wife (*The
Taming of the Shrew*)
One's bitten, two die (*Antony and Cleopatra*)
Italian court rules on meat-cut quotes (*The
Merchant of Venice*)
Teenage bride's suicide bluff misfires (*Romeo and
Juliet*)
Pensioner and three daughters die after 'You can't
stay here' row (*King Lear*)
March murder horror: victim ignored warnings
(*Julius Caesar*)
Hanky-panky puts paid to mixed marriage
(*Othello*)
'There are fairies in the garden of our Bottom'
claims drama star (*A Midsummer Night's
Dream*)
Deposed duke 'living in fantasy world' (*The
Tempest*)
Four die as fencing friendly gets out of hand
(*Hamlet*)

The greatest story ever sold

Children's book blurbs – a guide to interpretation

'Loved by generations of children': *Saw it first on television*
'The greatest story ever told': *Teenage Mutant Ninja Turtles*
'Babies love it': *Suck the pages*
'Award-winner': *About social problems*
'An exciting sequel': *Author dissuaded from writing anything original*
'A world of knowledge': *Another encyclopaedia*
'Collect the series': *We're not stupid*
'Immortal characters': *Orville and Cuddles*
'Cookery for children': *Mainly crushed digestive biscuits*
'For children of all ages': *Silly adults read it*

Ten characters with forgotten first names

Biggles (James)
Jeeves (Reginald)
Mr Magoo (Quincy)
Ivanhoe (Wilfred)
Moriarty (James)
Mr Chips (Arthur)
Little Lord Fauntleroy (Cedric)
Falstaff (Jack)
Dr Watson (John)
Rambo (John)

My name is Biggles, James Biggles

Great works of fiction ignored by the Booker Prize jury

Your last tax return
Your last expenses claim
Your current job application form
The guarantee card for your £3.99 watch
The next Labour/Conservative/Liberal Democrat manifesto
The estate agent's brochure pushed through your door
The *What's On* guide to Goole
The Lonely Hearts column
The official statement after a cabinet minister resigns
Sunday Sport's front page

A Noddy in the right direction – ten updated children's books

The Mineral Water Babies
Sub-Postman Patel
Swallows and Amazon Rainforests
The Lion, the Witch and the Self-Assembly
    Wardrobe
Alice in Disneyland
The Secret Garden Centre
Thomasina the Tank Engine
The Tale of Jason Rabbit
Alternative Physician Doolittle
Tom Chainsawyer

Ten acceptable excuses if caught in possession of a Jeffrey Archer novel

I'm a kleptomaniac
I'm an insomniac
I'm looking after it for a friend
Sorry, I no speaka de Engleesh
I got delayed at an airport
I've got *Remembrance of Things Past* hidden inside
    it
I'm a television executive
I'm doing a thesis on popular fiction
I swapped it for a broken elastic band
Somebody planted it on me

I wrote it – and that's my excuse

Start with an earthquake and build up to a climax – ten opening lines that make you want to read on

'As Gregor Samsa woke one morning from uneasy
    dreams he found himself transformed in his bed
    into a gigantic insect' (Franz Kafka,
    Metamorphosis)
'It was the afternoon of my 81st birthday, and I
    was in bed with my catamite when Ali
    announced that the archbishop had come to see
    me' (Anthony Burgess, *Earthly Powers*)
'Hale knew, before he had been in Brighton three
    hours, that they meant to murder him' (Graham
    Greene, *Brighton Rock*)
'I'm going to get that bloody bastard if I die in the
    attempt' (James Clavell, *King Rat*)
'It was a cold bright day in April, and the clocks
    were striking 13' (George Orwell, *1984*)
'Lolita, light of my life, fire of my loins, my sin, my
    soul' (Vladimir Nabokov, *Lolita*)
'Many years later, as he faced the firing squad,
    Colonel Aureliano Buendia was to remember
    that distant afternoon when his father took him
    to discover ice' (Gabriel Garcia Marquez, *One
    Hundred Years of Solitude*)
'I intensely disliked my father's fifth wife, but not
    to the point of murder' (Dick Francis, *Hot
    Money*)
'There were 117 psychoanalysts on the Pan Am
    flight to Vienna and I'd been treated by at least
    six of them' (Erica Jong, *Fear of Flying*)
' "Sent down for indecent behaviour, eh?" said
    Paul Pennyfather's guardian' (Evelyn Waugh,
    Decline and Fall)

Thriller-speak –
a guide to interpretation

'Post-*Glasnost* thriller': *Nobody knows which side they're on*

'Technothriller': *Most fully developed character is a nuclear submarine*

'More than just a thriller': *Also a wooden love story*

'From London and New York to Moscow and Peking': *Travelogue in case you get bored*

'Topical': *Based on five-year-old newspaper clipping*

'The ultimate nightmare': *Having to read the entire book*

'Non-stop adventure': *Seems to go on forever*

'Classic thriller': *Original conspiracy theory*

'Mysteries of the Orient': *Philosophy or sex, preferably both*

'Now a major motion picture': *Stars Sean Connery or Michael Caine*

Ten memorable characters from Beachcomber

Boubou Flaring (actress)
Scorpion de Rooftrouser (red-bearded dwarf)
Scrubby Botulos (boxing promotor)
Rustiguzzi (opera singer)
Stultitia Cabstanleigh (authoress)
Roland Milk (poet)
E W Whackfast (cabman)
Tinklebury Snapdriver (barrister)
Churm Rincewind (red-bearded dwarf)
Inspector Malpractice (policeman)

Romantic fiction –
a guide to interpretation

'She knew life would never be the same again': *At last, a dishwasher!*

'He possessed her utterly and totally': *He's hidden her Post Office savings book*

'Their bodies seemed to merge into one': *Nasty dip in the bed*

'There was a terrible, screaming emptiness': *Bognor promenade in winter*

'It was what she'd yearned for all these years and now it was hers': *A complete cookery partwork*

'His deep blue eyes misted over': *Dust in the contact lenses*

'Her eyes closed and her full, red lips parted': *About to sneeze*

'It was theirs now and for all eternity': *One week in a Florida timeshare*

'She trembled at his touch': *He really should do something about those cold hands*

'He transported her to ecstasies she never knew existed': *The all-day, American-style breakfast at the Little Chef*

MISCELLANY

Ten stages in the development of *homo sapiens*

Development of crude tools (*keys for opening sardine tins*)

Discovers fire (*ability to barbecue meat to a cinder on the outside, while leaving the inside totally uncooked*)

Simple sign language (*writing in the air with an imaginary pen when you want the bill in a restaurant*)

Rudimentary verbal communication (*Two pints of lager and a packet of crisps*)

Discovery of the wheel (*eventually leads to the discovery of the traffic jam*)

Builds basic shelter (*package holiday hotels*)

Gathers into communities for self-protection (*Freemasons*)

Turns from hunting to agriculture (*spends more time in the garden centre than Sainsbury's*)

Attempts at simplistic writing (*advertising copy for stretch covers*)

Sheds body hair (*Afghan coats go out of fashion*)

'Please speak after the tone . . .' Ten celebrity Ansaphone messages

'I'm not in at the moment, but I hope to be one day' (Neil Kinnock)

'I'm afraid we're all out – as usual' (Graham Gooch)

'There's no one to answer your call as we're all tied up' (Cynthia Payne)

'I can't talk right now – but then I've never been able to' (Sylvester Stallone)

'When you hear the bleeps, you'll know I'm doing my act' (Dave Allen)

'I'm out – and came out some time ago' (Sir Ian McKellen)

'Leave your name, number, the time you called, age, hair colour and vital statistics' (Warren Beatty)

'I'm unavailable at present, but why don't you call me in a couple of weeks?' (Cher)

'I'm not here, but why should any of us be here?' (Woody Allen)

'I'm out, but I'll be back after the break' (Sir Alastair Burnet)

Ten(uous) excuses for speeding

I was rushing to get to the petrol station before my tank ran out

I was rushing to get to the petrol station before the free lead crystal glasses ran out

I'm a member of the royal family

I'm a research physicist trying to prove Einstein's theory of relativity

Thank heavens, officer, I thought the flashing blue light chasing me was a UFO

My shoes have just been re-soled and I'm not used to the extra weight

I've got a new in-car air freshener and was in a complete daze

I was trying to reach my destination before Rabbi Lionel Blue came on the radio

Those go-faster stripes really do work, then

I was trying to make up the hour we lost when the clocks went forward

Know your limit – ten tell-tale signs that you might have drunk too much

Waking up in the middle of the night clutching a Chinese spare rib

Doing a karaoke version of *Ruby Don't Take Your Love to Town*

Trying to take your trousers off over your head

Over-ordering outrageously in an Indian restaurant

Pouring Lucozade on your cornflakes

Ringing your wife at two in the morning to say you love her

Telling your best mate that you love him

Waking up in railway sidings at Crewe

Giving the taxi driver a £5 tip

Trying to juggle with peanuts

Who says you're too old to work? Ten jobs for senior citizens

Model for zip-up cardigans

Delivery driver for Morris Minors

Stunt woman for Joan Collins

Chairlift demonstrator

Bouncer at a Women's Institute produce sale

Roadie for Val Doonican

President of the USA

Guru to the Prince of Wales

An extra in *The Golden Girls*

Whist drive promoter

Ten questions to make the kids squirm

Are you doing anything about those spots?
Guess what I found in your bedroom today?
Why do your clothes smell of smoke?
Are you planning to stay in bed all day?
Have you thought about trying contact lenses?
Would you like to come out to the front and
    explain how you got that answer?
Just what has happened to your dinner money?
What are you doing up there?
Have you been wearing make-up?
Do you know anything about this broken window?

There's no answer to that –
ten mysteries of life

How can you look up the spelling of a word if you
    can't spell it?
Why do dogs always think it's for them when
    there's a knock at the door?
Why does the sun turn you brown but your sofa
    white?
Was the education system invented merely to give
    us something to talk about at dinner parties?
How do we know that God likes hymns?
Where do good television programmes go in the
    summer?
Why are veins blue when blood is red?
What have skulls got to grin about?
Why are all American TV news reporters called
    Bob?
If one in every three people is Chinese, why are
    Bananarama all English?

The real meaning of ten clichés

'A snail's pace': *0.031mph*
'Knee high to a grasshopper': *2.5cm*
'Not worth a fig': *One fresh fig costs around 50p*
'Breeds like a rabbit': *A litter of five or six every 30
    days*
'Quick as a flash': *Lightning travels between 100
    and 1,000 miles per second*
'Went like a bullet': *A .22 calibre cartridge travels
    at 331 metres per second*
'Like watching paint dry': *16 hours for gloss paint*
'Once in a blue moon': *The last blue moon seen
    over Britain was in September 1950*
'As straight as an arrow': *61 metres per second*
'Light as a feather ': *A down duck feather weighs
    0.05oz*

Ten tough questions for *Mastermind* contestants

Where were you when Ronald Reagan was shot?

Who is your Euro MP?

What is your National Insurance number?

Who won last year's Eurovision Song Contest?

Name the title of a Barbara Cartland novel

What do you call those white strips of plastic used for stirring coffee?

Where did you put the guarantee card for the washing machine?

Name a film starring Zsa Zsa Gabor

Explain how the divisional play-offs work at the end of the football season

Are you ready for 1992?

Who could forget *A Virgin in Mayfair*?

Lipstick on your collar – ten creative excuses

It's actually a pink shirt with a giant white stain

A woman tried to give the kiss of life to a dying moth on my collar

I was mistaken for the Blarney Stone

I thought it would go well with the tie

I was standing next to an Avon Lady when her handbag exploded

My secretary needed somewhere to wipe her mouth after lunch

My shirt is having an affair

It helps me to remember which way up the shirt goes

I'm taking an evening class in tribal warpaint

Damn, the sales assistant warned me it might be shop-soiled

There's nothing worse than . . .

Putting on a polo neck jumper that isn't quite dry

The music they play on TV when there's a technical fault

The intermission between the adverts and the film at a cinema

The smell from mobile hamburger stands

Men with long fingernails

The hairdryer breaking down half-way through doing your hair

Emptying the fluff from a vacuum cleaner bag

Waiters not filling in the bottom of your credit card slip when service is already included in the bill

The changing room floors at swimming pools

Saturday night television

And they call it puppy love – ten tell-tale signs

Holding hands in the supermarket
Reading each other's horoscopes
Getting one milk shake and two straws
Wearing each other's sweaters
Dancing cheek-to-cheek to heavy metal bands
Phoning each other six times a day
Finding an anniversary to celebrate every week
Being embarrassed about going to the loo
Writing to each other even when you're not apart
Having 'your song'

Ten couples who were made for each other

Smith & Jones (Maggie and Tom)
Abbott & Costello (Diane and Elvis)
Cannon & Ball (Dyan and Alan)
Bryant & May (David and Elaine)
Black & Decker (Conrad and Carol)
Johnson & Johnson (Jilly and Don)
Bull & Bush (Steve and Kate)
Sid & Nancy (Lawrence and Reagan)
Lilley & Skinner (Peter and Dennis)
Bill & Ben (Cosby and Elton)

Ten things that make you feel grown up

Having breakfast before opening your presents on
   Christmas Day
Buying a classical record
Offering to buy the pub landlord a drink
Knowing a doctor socially
Having a party where the drink doesn't run out
Travelling alone on a plane
Meeting your child's teacher
Receiving your very own junk mail
Checking into an hotel
Having your parents round to dinner

Take two large lips . . .

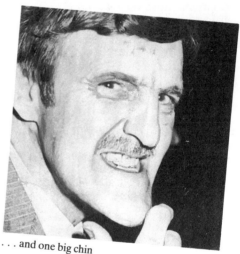

. . . and one big chin

Make your own monster – ten bits you'll need

Gérard Dépardieu's nose
Norman Lamont's eyes
Denis Healey's eyebrows
Mick Jagger's lips
Janet Street-Porter's teeth
Jimmy Hill's chin
Roy Hattersley's cheeks
Shane McGowan's ears
Ken Dodd's hair
Mike Tyson's neck

Ten things which can only be found in Christmas crackers

A deformed plastic Red Indian

The left-hand side of a paper hat

A circular piece of card with a broken elastic band attached to it

A whistle which is audible only to South American fruitbats

A celluloid fish which tells your fortune

A riddle that was unfunny in 1923

An alphabet game with only 17 letters

A miniature water pistol without a hole in the nozzle

A spinning top with razor-sharp edges

A pink plastic compass the size of a shirt button

Ten New Year's resolutions you never keep

To write in your diary every day

To make a note of where you put the Christmas decorations

To spend less time reading the Sunday papers

To learn a foreign language

To tidy your desk every night before going home

To go away for Christmas next year

To start writing a novel

To finish the one you started reading this year

To do something about the damp patch in the bathroom

To give up making resolutions

If she married him, the result would be . . .

Ali McGraw and Chris Barber (Ali Barber)

Rustie Lee and Jimmy Nail (Rustie Nail)

Mynah Bird and John Major (Mynah Major)

Brooke Shields and Alan Bond (Brooke Bond)

Rose Tremain and George Bush (Rose Bush)

Toni Basil and Herbie Hancock (Toni Hancock)

Crystal Gale and Philip Glass (Crystal Glass)

Goldie Hawn and Michael Fish (Goldie Fish)

Jerry Hall and Tony Adams (Jerry Adams)

Brogan Lane and Terry Wogan (Brogan Wogan)

Towards the millennium – ten things to look forward to in the year 2000

Accrington's year as European City of Culture

The Prince Edward Players present *When Did You Last See Your Trousers?*

Frank Sinatra's thirtieth annual farewell tour: *One Man and his Zimmer*

Commercials for the re-privatisation of electricity

The Golden Age of Jeremy Beadle Exhibition at the British Museum

The Harry Enfield Christmas Variety Show

The Janet Street-Porter Reith Lectures (simultaneous translation into English)

Dudley Moore finding his Tesco chickens

Sir Gazza

Grand opening ceremony for the Channel Tunnel

No, Sir Gazza, you can't keep the sword

Initial thoughts – an alternative view

DIY: Destroy It Yourself
RSC: Really Strapped for Cash
GB: Going Broke
BAA: Baggage at Another Airport
CIA: Caught In the Act
KGB: Knife Gorby in the Back
NUM: Never Underestimate Militants
CEGB: Cash Excess Generating Board
CAP: Costs A Packet
PMT: Pre-Match Tension

Curry . . .

. . . and Rice

Ten dishy couples

James Brown and Barbara Windsor
John Curry and Anneka Rice
Michael Fish and Chips Channon
Alan Sugar and Marc Almond
Dawn French and Andy Bean
Peaches Geldof and Lol Creme
Jack Lemmon and David Soul
Francis Bacon and The Earl of Sandwich
Rock Hudson and Jamie Salmon
Allan Lamb and Christopher Chope

Ten greetings cards they're still working on

Good Luck In Your New Sweater
Our Prayers Go Out To You On The Arrival Of
    Your Gas Bill
Hope Your Pen Turns Up Soon
Merry Ramadan
So Pleased You Got Home In Time For *Bergerac*
Congratulations On Your 21st Penalty Point
To Both Of You On Your Decree Nisi
Pancake Day Greetings
Sorry I Forgot Your Ansaphone Message
Keep Your Chin Up At The War Crimes Trial

Count your blessings . . .

Morris dancing is not part of the National
    Curriculum
Loyd Grossman has another five million homes to
    inspect before he gets round to yours
For most of your life you won't look like your
    passport photograph
One day children will ask: 'Turtles? What are
    they?'
Belgians rarely go abroad
Nobody has ever died from acne
Daytime TV happens when you're at work
Kitty Kelley has absolutely no interest in your life
    story
Nobody talks about house prices any more
Bill Wyman hasn't met your teenage daughter

Old people – a guide to interpretation

'A real character': *Sits in the pub and waits to be bought drinks*
'Still all there': *Obstinate*
'Always cheerful': *Keeps her ailments to herself*
'Marvellous for her age': *Still eating solids*
'Sense of humour': *Pretends to be deaf*
'Feisty': *Cooks own Pot Noodles*
'Amazing memory': *About anything that happened before 1930*
'Never complains': *Wouldn't dare*
'Independent': *Sends Meals on Wheels away*
'Keeps active': *Frightens the kids next door*

Ten things which lurk at the back of the wardrobe

An empty shoe box
A broken tennis racket
A plastic belt
A pair of split leather shoes
An old woollen blanket
Your collections of 1960s singles
A knitted tie
A university scarf
An airline bag
A cardboard tube

Ten things you wish you'd never started

A doorstep conversation with a salesman
Plumbing in a shower
Cutting your own hair
A 21-day wonder diet
Flirting with the next-door neighbour
Trying out a sample of carpet shampoo
The third bottle of wine
A complete medical check-up
Looking for dry rot in the loft
A Dance to the Music of Time

It makes you think – why is it that . . .

Chinese restaurants can produce any one of 300 dishes within five minutes?

Sir David Steel and Meatloaf have never appeared together on *Question Time*?

Lada dealers are always at the top of hills?

Television chefs never eat the food they cook?

Most cinema managers are bald?

Prisoner: Cell Block H is shown only after everyone has gone to bed?

Arnold Schwarzenegger and Sylvester Stallone have never appeared in pantomime?

Pet shops are next door to fast food restaurants?

Moira Stuart always gets stuck with working weekends?

There are more ads on TV for women shaving than men?

Applying for a new job?
Ten things to omit from your CV

The name of your probation officer

Your favourite character in *EastEnders*

Your recipe for French dressing

Your membership number of the Dennis the Menace fan club

The colour of your new bathroom suite

Your tip for the Derby

Your top ten *Carry On* films

The names of your pet fish

Your all-time England Cricket XI

Your hat size

The history of the world in ten odd museums

The Water Supply Museum of the City of Vienna (Austria)

The Resist US Aggression and Aid Korea Movement Museum (China)

The Stove-Plate Museum of the Swabian Ironworks (Germany)

The Man from Snowy River Museum (Australia)

The Professor Dr Van Den Poel Museum of Taxation (Holland)

The Museum of Frying Pan Making (France)

The Museum of Travelling on Foot (Austria)

The De Platjin Museum of Clogs (Holland)

The Billiards Museum (Australia)

The Wallpaper Museum (France)

Hospital-speak –
a guide to interpretation

'The operation was a success': *We've got the same number of instruments as when we started*

'He is now back in the ward': *We lost him for a couple of hours*

'He feels very weak': *Our policy of waking him up at five every morning is working*

'He's in a stable condition': *Feels like he's been kicked by a horse*

'He is comfortable': *Not been in long enough to develop bedsores*

'He is alert': *Keeps showing everyone his operation scar*

'Is able to receive visitors': *Can't stop him talking*

'Responding well': *Trying to chat up the nurses*

'Showing definite signs of his old self': *Caught smoking in the toilets*

'Should be able to go home soon': *He's starting to give medical advice to the doctors*

If she married him, the result would be . . .

Whoopi Goldberg and Peter Cushing (Whoopi Cushing)
Cher and Noddy Holder (Cher Holder)
Kitty Kelley and Conway Twitty (Kitty Twitty)
Cyd Charisse and Rich Little (Cyd Little)
Mae West and Robin Day (Mae Day)
Jessica Lange and Eddie Rabbitt (Jessica Rabbitt)
Sandie Shaw and Timothy Bottoms (Sandie Bottoms)
Tuesday Weld and Andrew Knight (Tuesday Knight)
Cherie Lunghi and Oliver Stone (Cherie Stone)
Robin Givens and Jeff Banks (Robin Banks)

A marriage made . . .

. . . in the City

It makes you think – ten more mysteries of life

If moths are so attracted to light, why don't they come out during the day?
Why is there no ham in hamburgers?
What is the second line of the song *Guantanamera*?
Why do people say 'Sorry' when you tread on their feet?
Why are other people's newspapers so fascinating?
Why are square boxing arenas called rings?
Why do all newborn babies look like Elton John?
How come your skin leaks out but not in?
Why does slow up mean the same as slow down?
Why are camouflage jackets so conspicuous?

No kidding – ten excuses for not having a baby

'We've just decorated and it might clash with the wallpaper'
'Our nanny values her independence too much'
'We'd prefer to replace our album collection with CDs first'
'There's a danger it might bring us closer together'
'We wouldn't want the budgie to get jealous'
'We wouldn't want to land a modern child with the stigma of coming from a two-parent family'
'I wouldn't want to be responsible for perpetuating my mother-in-law's genes'
'Those romantic nights – we'd have to have one'
'We're waiting for them to bring out a drip-dry version'
'If we wanted something chubby and drooling, we'd adopt Roy Hattersley'

Are you one of us or one of them? Ten things on which the world divides

The Beatles or the Stones
John or Paul
Hard or soft centres
Breakfast TV or radio
Marzipan
John Motson or Brian Moore
Cats or dogs
Dinner as the midday or evening meal
Coke or Pepsi
Poirot or Miss Marple

Are you past it? Ten tell-tale signs

Dialling long-distance wears you out
You sit in a rocking chair and can't make it work
A gypsy offers to read your face
Your favourite bit of the newspaper is '50 years ago today'
The old lady you help across the street is your wife
You wear as much clothing in bed as you do out
You can't work out how to find Radio 2 on FM
You never manage to make it through the whole of *News at Ten*
Sweet sherry doesn't seem so bad
Your knees buckle, but your belt won't

A beginner's guide to American

'Revenue enhancement': *Tax increases*
'Inoperative statements': *Lies*
'Fourth-quarter equity retreat': *Stock-market crash*
'Ambient non-combatant personnel': *Vietnamese refugees*
'Pavement deficiencies': *Potholes*
'Negative patient care outcome': *Death due to medical malpractice*
'Involuntary conversion of a 727': *Plane crash*
'Members of a career offender cartel': *Mafia*
'Urban transportation specialists': *Taxi drivers*
'Environmental technicians': *Janitors*

Ten things to do with that Comic Relief red nose

Donate it to the local Oxfam shop
Return it to Sir Alastair Burnet
Keep a pet tadpole in it
Put it back in the cotton wool for next time (Scotland only)
Use it as a spot cosy
Paint it black and wear it at funereal occasions (e.g. England cricket matches)
Use it to top off your knickerbocker glory impression
Convert it into a bonsai hanging basket
Add it to the European Community red nose mountain
Give it to a reindeer

Whatever you do, give it plenty of fresh air

Why, oh, why?
Ten great philosophical questions

Why is there always one teaspoon left in the bowl after you've done the washing-up?

Why does grass smell only when you mow it?

Why is there always a coffee stain on page 63 of your library book?

Why can you never buy a bottle of shampoo without 25 per cent extra in it?

Why is there no heating outside, where it's really cold?

Why is it considered necessary to nail down the lid of a coffin?

Why did Shakespeare use so many famous quotations in his work?

Why does a ringing telephone take precedence over everything else in the known universe?

Why do floorboards creak only after midnight?

Why do butterflies live for such a short time, when eating cabbage is supposed to be so healthy?

Ten entries in the upper-class dictionary

Freight: *A sudden shock*

Cosh: *Vulgar method of settling one's accaints*

'Excess cod': *Super plastic thingy for paying bills*

Ace: *The frozen lumpy bits in one's drinky-poos*

Shah: *What one has in one's investment portfolio*

Celery: *Frightfully useful thing one can swap for shahs*

Eight: *Not in*

Par: *What the GTi has a lot of under the bonnet*

Cake: *Illegal white substance taken at all the best parties*

Bed: *Hairy growth that one's analyst has on his chin*

The first cuckoo –
ten signs that spring is on the way

Women's magazines suggest that you look at yourself naked

Your child demands a live chick for Easter

'Winter Sale Must End' signs are replaced by 'Fabulous Spring Sale' signs

Liverpool are way ahead at the top of the Football League

Plastic donkeys with pannier baskets appear in front gardens

A young man's fancy turns to cricket practice

Shops start stocking up with anoraks for next winter

There are traffic jams at the garden centre

The world is full of ads for lawn mowers

It snows

Ten protected species (worth saving for their names alone)

Trembling Sea-Mat

Glutinous Snail

Wart-Biter Grasshopper

Small Alison

Martin's Ramping-Fumitory

Drooping Saxifrage

Dickie's Bladder Fern

Stinking Hawk's-Beard

Creeping Marshwort

Stinking Goosefoot

Ten childish questions guaranteed to flummox parents

Why is there snow on mountains when they're nearer the sun?

Why are seas salty when the rivers that flow into them are fresh?

Why doesn't your stomach digest itself?

How did the first man to look in a mirror recognise himself?

If there are 7 days in a week and 52 weeks in a year, why are there 365 days a year?

Why does coloured soap make white bubbles?

Who does God believe in?

How can amnesia victims still remember how to talk?

Why don't you shrink after taking a bath?

Why don't fish drown?

'This sounds like a job for . . .' Ten super-heroes for the 1990s

Captain Cellnet
The Incredible Bag Lady
Armchair Strategist
The Phantom Car Clamper
Lead-Free Man
Timeshare Woman
Sunday Trader
The Glass Re-Cycler
Inflation Fighter
The Mortgage Re-Negotiator

Ten classical gods given a new lease of life

Pan: God of theatre critics
Diana: Goddess of the media
Thor: God of burst pipes
Bacchus: God of horse-racing
Poseidon: God of Christmas films on TV
Mars: God of work, rest and play
Juno: Goddess of gossip
Flora: Goddess of dieting
Nike: God of torn ligaments
Vulcan: God of Trekkies

Designer lapels – ten badge slogans

Help the aged: loosen sauce bottle tops
My other back passage is a porch
The lions of Longleat have seen me
I think, therefore I, er . . . need a headache tablet
I'm innocent – this badge was pinned on me
This human being was pinned on me
I may be small, but I scare spiders
Help! I'm being held prisoner in a badge factory
Beaver-infested rivers are just one dam thing after
    another
Why join the army when you can be a Leeds
    United supporter?

Don't waste space –
ten creative brainstorms

Vladivar Vodka was advertised on the sides of
    cows grazing alongside the London to Brighton
    railway line
Ready Brek was advertised on children's exercise
    books in Strathclyde schools
Williams Furniture was advertised on the
    waistband of Muhammad Ali's boxing shorts
Saatchi and Saatchi advertised themselves on the
    Berlin Wall
Highland Silk Whisky was advertised on the sides
    of sheep at a sheep-dog trial
Simoniz sports goods were advertised on the
    bottom of the pool at the European diving
    championships
Rumbelows were advertised on banners fluttering
    from the ends of the pole carried by high wire
    artist Steve McPeak as he balanced 1,500 feet
    above Rio de Janeiro
Coca-Cola was advertised on wire netting strung
    between palm trees over rice fields in the
    Philippines
James Capel, stockbrokers, were advertised
    around the necks of Remy Martin bottles
Saga Holidays were advertised on OAP bus tickets
    in Manchester

Remember, remember –
the ten laws of Bonfire Night

Next door's firework display is always more
    exciting
The catherine wheel is guaranteed to fly off the
    tree
It if doesn't, it spins once and then gets stuck
The firework you save till the end is a big
    disappointment
The fire fizzles out before you've had time to cook
    the baked potatoes
The milk bottle falls over just as the biggest rocket
    is about to take off
Boys want to light bangers, but end up holding
    sparklers
Someone loses a filling in a toffee apple
Your lawn is never the same again
Everyone agrees it was a total waste of money

Ten new patron saints

St Michael: Patron saint of dinner parties
St Bruno: Patron saint of bad breath
St Malo: Patron saint of duty frees
St Leger: Patron saint of bookmakers
St Laurent: Patron saint of advertising executives
St Albans: Patron saint of commuters
St John: Patron saint of soccer pundits
St Moritz: Patron saint of orthopaedic surgeons
St Ivel: Patron saint of fridge manufacturers
St Ives: Patron saint of wet weekends

Pardon my French – a beginner's guide

'Entente cordiale': *A drink in the sponsor's marquee*
'Nouveau': *Fresh veal*
'Pied-à-terre': *Tricky things these French urinals*
'Arc de Triomphe': *A winning smile*
'Lire': *To read a dirty book*
'Après': *After the church service*
'Aller': *To proceed down a narrow street*
'Malade': *A sick duck*
'Pièce de résistance': *An unsuccessful first date*
'Oeuf': *A horse's foot*

And what's yours called?

What's in a name?
Ten children who'll find out

Dakota Mayi (Don Johnson and Melanie Griffith)
Story (Chris Difford)
Statten (Nicolas Roeg and Theresa Russell)
Samuel Hurricane (Dave Stewart and Siobhan Fahey)
Harley Moon (Martin Kemp and Shirlie Holliman)
Langley Fox (Mariel Hemingway)
Free (Barbara Hershey)
Saethryd Charity (Gyles Brandreth)
Aphra Kendal (Gyles Brandreth)
Rain (Richard Pryor)

Ten terms from the Trabant drivers' manual

'Trabanter': *Chit-chat about cars*
'Trabantique': *Classic car*
'Trabantwerp': *Driver*
'Trabantifreeze': *Heavy overcoat worn by trabantwerps*
'Trabantimacassar': *Seat cover*
'Trabantenna': *Radio aerial*
'Trabanthea': *Woman driver*
'Trabantisocial': *Emptying ashtrays in the gutter*
'Trabandoned': *Breakdown on the motorway*
'Trabantiknock': *Taking the Trabant seriously*

Communication breakdown – ten words which could get us into trouble in Europe

Mist (German): Manure
Baby foot (French): Table football
Mug (Danish): Mildew
Bribe (French): Scrap
Hell (Norwegian): Success
Fart (Swedish): Road travel
Tit (Danish): Often
Mad (Danish): Food
Kiss (Swedish): Pee
Gift (German): Poison

With a name like Gyles, wouldn't you exact revenge?

'Ooh, Betty' – 'Next'

That big interview – ten things which might just cost you the job

Turning up three months late
Taking your mum with you
Calling the interviewer 'pal' or 'squire'
Letting your ice-cream drip on the carpet
Referring to the company's product as 'thingummibobs'
Periodically affecting a Frank Spencer voice for comic relief
Listening to your Walkman
Extinguishing your cigarette by dropping it in your tea
Extinguishing your cigarette by dropping it in the interviewer's tea
Eating all the chocolate biscuits and leaving the interviewer the digestives

Ten things you always think of too late

A devastatingly witty reply
Buying Christmas presents during the summer sales
Keeping your original Beatles singles
Making a will
Taking your umbrella
Checking to see if there's enough toilet paper
Sending postcards on a one-week holiday
Filling the ice trays before a party
Changing the alarm when the clocks go forward
Drawing up a pre-marital contract

Ten embarrassing holiday destinations

Condom (*France*)
Aars (*Denmark*)
Prattville (*USA*)
Bastad (*Sweden*)
Dire (*Mali*)
Bitche (*France*)
Finke (*Australia*)
Spittal (*Austria*)
Blacksod (*Eire*)
Hell (*Cayman Islands*)

Can't sleep? Ten things to do at four o'clock in the morning

Count the Artex ripples on the ceiling
Call First Direct
See if you can find any faces in the chintz curtains
Go to work and avoid the rush hour
Phone someone in Australia
Browse through your children's pop magazines
Listen to John Peel on the World Service
Try to find your house insurance policy
Rearrange your bookshelves alphabetically
Think up ideas for *Journolists*

The golden age of marketing – ten mail order ads from 100 years ago

Caxton's Patent Ear-Cap (3/6d): *'For remedying prominent ears, preventing disfigurement in after life, keeps the hair tidy (send measure round head just above ears)'*

Hieratica Mourning Envelopes (1/6d per 100): *'The Ancient writing paper of the priests'*

Towel's Pennyroyal & Steel Pills for Females (2/10d in stamps): *'Quickly correct all irregularities, remove all obstructions, and relieve the distressing symptoms so prevalent with the sex'*

Dewar's Choice Old Whisky (£1 19s for two gallons): *'A combination of the finest whiskies made in the Highlands of Scotland, thoroughly matured in wood after sherry, for family use'*

Invigorator Corsets (Boys & Girls 7/6d): *The Countess of Suffolk says, August 26, 1890, "I think them such good stays, and those you sent for my daughter answered admirably" '*

Second Quality Oxidised Keyless Watch (£2 2s): *'Silver initial set with diamonds'*

Deane's Hygienic Domestic Folding Hot-Air and Vapour Bath Cabinet (£1 10s): *'A message of hope to suffering humanity (folds up when not in use)'*

Ritter Road Skates (£3 15s): *'Healthful, fashionable and charming (when ordering, send outline of boot on paper)'*

Patent Canvas House Shoe (2/9d): *'Will last for nearly 12 months with ordinary daily wear. Absorbs perspiration readily. Recommended by The Lancet for "Cold and Tender Feet" '*

Campbell's Paragon Melodeons (14/-): *'The solemn psalm, the soul-stirring hymn, the cheerful song and the merry dance can all be played on these charming instruments. No knowledge of music is required by the player'*

Ten things you can find in a fruit bowl

A blunt pencil
A free sachet of moisturising cream
A mysterious key
A money-off coupon for a new lavatory cleaner
Pebbles from days out at the beach
An ancient walnut
A charity envelope (empty)
Two buttons
A box of promotional matches
A small plastic toy (broken)

Ten old words which are worth reviving

Bedswerver: an unfaithful spouse
Bellibone: a beautiful young girl
Chantpleure: to sing and weep at the same time
Fellowfeel: to empathise with
Lip-clap: a kiss
Lubberwart: food with little or no nutritional value
Mubblefubbles: melancholy feelings
Poplolly: a mistress or lover
Prickmedainty: a dedicated follower of fashion
Smellsock: a lecher

Whatever happened to the lambada? Ten dances to take its place

The Cabinet Shuffle
The No Can-Can Do
The Prince Charleston
The Waltz Disney
The Oliver Twist
The Desmond Morris Dance
The Samantha Foxtrot
The Diana Quickstep
The Charles Dance
The Opinion Polka

It takes two to tango, Sam

Ten people who are known by their middle names

Charles Robert Redford
James Paul McCartney
Patrick Ryan O'Neal
Cuthbert Gordon Greenidge
Michael Terence Wogan
Robert Oliver Reed
John Enoch Powell
Keith Rupert Murdoch
Sir Peter Norman Fowler
Michael Sylvester Stallone

Robert . . .

. . . and Keith

The European capitals in the USA

London (Kentucky)
Lisbon (North Dakota)
Athens (Michigan)
Vienna (Mississippi)
Paris (Arkansas)
Madrid (Iowa)
Rome (Georgia)
Dublin (Texas)
Amsterdam (Ohio)
Oslo (Minnesota)

Playbill-speak – putting those quotes into context

'A remarkable achievement': *It's a remarkable achievement that this kind of rubbish still gets produced*

'Gripping': *It's as gripping as a ten-year-old car tyre*

'Had the audience on its feet': *It had the audience on its feet in the stampede for the exits*

'Packed every night': *After half an hour of the performance, the theatre bar is packed every night*

'The most glittering show in town': *When I saw it in Goole, it was the most glittering show in town*

'The audience cheered loudly': *When the set collapsed, the audience cheered loudly*

'I can't recommend it enough': *I can't recommend it – enough said*

'An outstanding performance': *We all remember his outstanding performance last year*

'Full of great songs': *The show is full of great songs, but the singing is atrocious*

'Will run and run': *Audiences will run and run from this one*

Ten things nobody admits to

Letting their children watch as much TV as they want
Being unable to take a joke at their own expense
Being bored by the latest news from Eastern Europe
Being the guilty party in a car accident
Being a rotten lover
Being a Sylvester Stallone fan
Being a back-seat driver
The amount they earn
Being the 'average man in the street'
Not caring about elephants

Ten things which aren't worth recycling (yet)

Nail clippings
Party poppers
Pencil shavings
The stuffing from padded envelopes
Cigarette ends
Used Sellotape
Cocktail sticks
The peel-off strips on the back of plasters
Olive stones
Maureen Lipman's magazine columns

The G-plan diet – ten easy steps to weight loss

Arrange for your salary to be paid in carrots
Donate an organ
Weigh yourself outside the earth's atmosphere
Use woodchip wallpaper instead of cheese slices
Wear lighter hats
Buy all the slimming magazines you can – and eat them
Put a picture of Liz Taylor on your fridge door
Restrict yourself to food which is past its sell-by date
Cut out pasta dishes between meals
Convert to polystyrene

Ten companionable drinking partners

Jim Beam (US parallel bars champion)
Tio Pepe (poodle parlour proprietor)
Remy Martin (international starlet)
Pils Lager (Danish speed skating champion, 1937)
Johnnie Walker (ageing DJ)
Lutomer Riesling (this month's Romanian foreign minister)
Jack Daniels (Southern US senator)
Bols Advocaat (Dutch soccer player)
Glen Fiddich (alternative Scottish comedian)
Rose D'Anjou (moody nightclub chanteuse)

Stars and cars

Audi Murphy
Toyota Wilcox
Austin Mitchell
Morgan Fairchild
Sierra Kennedy
Orion O'Neal
Lancia Percival
Yugo Montenegro
Astra Gilberto
Mercedes McCambridge

Was it worth it, Simon?

If only we'd known – where ten great inventions ultimately led

The gramophone: *Simon Bates*
The internal combustion engine: *Junk mail from the A.A*
The flush toilet: *Arguments about spending too long in the bathroom*
The printing press: *'Windsurfers Do It Standing Up' stickers*
The electric light: *Teak-effect bedside tables*
The steam engine: *Staff shortages*
The sewerage system: *Teenage Mutant Ninja Turtles*
The jet engine: *You in Paris, your luggage in Pisa*
The camera: *Other people's holiday snaps*
The telephone: *The portable telephone*

The real meaning of ten more clichés

'Snug as a bug in a rug': *Up to 60,000 dust mites lurk in each square yard of carpet*

'Busy as a bee': *The population of a hive have to fly 50,000 miles and visit four million flowers to make just one pound of honey*

'As old as Methuselah': *969 years*

'A heartbeat away': *0.83 seconds*

'Within spitting distance': *The world record for spitting a cherry stone is 72ft 7½ins*

'Eats like a vulture': *The vultures at London Zoo eat 3lb of meat a day*

'Blind as a bat': *Bats actually have very good eyesight*

'Astronomically high': *One astronomical unit is the average distance between the Earth and the Sun i.e. 92,955,807 miles*

'Like painting the Forth Bridge': *It takes 16 painters 6 years to repaint the bridge, using 17 tons of paint a year*

'High as a kite': *The highest altitude reached by a single kite is 12,471ft*

Simon, a capital guy